Tales from Ancient Egypt

The cover image by John Fisher features the enchanted prince and his bride. Here the prince is pointing to an image of Hathor, the Egyptian goddess who assigns a person's fates. This border of a wall painting containing the images of Hathor was discovered in the ancient palace at Nuzi near modern Kirkuk, Iraq. The Egyptian presence in the north was a dominant factor in the development of Ancient Mediterranean Literature.

Tales from Ancient Egypt

The Birth of Stories

TRANSLATED FROM THE EGYPTIAN

Loren R. Fisher

CASCADE *Books* • Eugene, Oregon

TALES FROM ANCIENT EGYPT
The Birth of Stories

Cascade Books
An Imprint of Wipf and Stock Publishers
199 W. 8th Ave., Suite 3
Eugene, OR 97401

www.wipfandstock.com

ISBN 13: 978-1-60608-657-5

Cataloging-in-Publication data:

Fisher, Loren R.
      Tales from ancient Egypt : the birth of stories / Loren R. Fisher.

      xiv + 100 p. ; cm. Includes bibliographical references and indexes.

      ISBN 13: 978-1-60608-657-5

      1. Egyptian literature—Translations into English. 2. Egypt—
Civilization—To 332 B.C. I. Title.

PJ1943 .F5 2010

Manufactured in the U.S.A.

For Jane

The *Ba* said,
"Reject the West;
Cling to life;
Love me here."
We said, "Yes."

Look, Amon made thunder in the sky,
when in his time, he put Seth beside him.
Indeed, Amon has established all the lands.
When he established them,
he established first the Land of Egypt
from which you have come.
Thus craftsmanship came from it
to reach the place where I am, and wisdom.

THE WORDS OF ZAKAR-BAAL, PRINCE OF BYBLOS,
FROM *THE JOURNEY OF WEN-AMON*

Contents

Preface ix

Acknowledgments xiii

Abbreviations xiv

Introduction 1

1 The Story of Sinuhe: A Wanderer on the Earth 5

2 The Enchanted Prince 30

3 The Story of the Shipwrecked Sailor 43

4 The Journey of Wen-Amon 54

5 A Dialogue between a Man and His *Ba* 73

Conclusion 85

Bibliography 93

Index of Authors and Scholars 97

Index of Ancient Documents 99

Preface

As a generalist in ancient Mediterranean studies with an emphasis on Northwest Semitic languages, I have also enjoyed my studies in Egyptian literature; these studies are not only helpful but also entertaining and fun. My appreciation for all things Egyptian, during my student days at Brandeis, was increased by the insights and enthusiasm of my friend William A. Ward. He remained helpful throughout his long tenure as an Egyptologist at The American University of Beirut. Egyptologists do not agree in their translations or interpretations of these stories, and my translations of these five stories are not intended to replace other translations. Rather translating is the means by which I can gain a better understanding of these stories,[1] and it provides the opportunity for me to enter into the discussion. I suggest that all readers consult other translations as well as the works listed in the bibliography.

These five Egyptian stories are extremely important. They are essential for comparative studies between the literature of the Hebrew Bible and the literature of the east Mediterranean world, and their importance for the study

1. This better understanding enabled me to give them a new setting in my novels: Fisher, *The Jerusalem Academy*, *The Minority Report*, and the forthcoming *Extending Horizons*.

of the beginnings of world literature cannot be overemphasized. Ancient Sumer and Egypt have given us writings earlier than these prose stories, but these five stories from second-millennium-BCE Egypt are representative of the oldest known literature specifically written for entertainment and adventure. They also provide subsequent storytellers with a long list of reoccurring themes, plots, and motifs. Those who study the history of world literature need to be aware that their story begins in Egypt, but many students have been deprived of this knowledge. Even celebrated critics have not appreciated the role of these ancient stories.

Adam Gopnik has an interesting essay in *The New Yorker* on C. S. Lewis.[2] There are many important parts to this essay, but I would like to focus my remarks on Gopnik's statement that Lewis's *The Allegory of Love* is his best book. It may be his best book, but from what Lewis says in a lengthy quote by Gopnik, I am troubled. In this quote, Lewis argues that before the Renaissance a writer only had access to "the actual world of experience and the world of religion." After the "Renaissance" a third world was added: "free mythological invention in which you did not need to believe." Lewis continues, "The probable, the marvelous-taken-as-fact, the marvelous-known-to-fiction—such is the triple equipment of the post-Renaissance poet . . . But this triple heritage is a late conquest. Go back to the beginnings of any literature and you will not find it."[3] Perhaps he is correct, because the earliest texts from Sumer and Egypt do not give us these

2. Gopnik, "Prisoner of Narnia," 88–93.
3. Ibid., 91.

stories, but autobiographical adventures and stories for entertainment stand at the beginning of the history of world literature long before Lewis's "Renaissance." "The Story of the Shipwrecked Sailor" is a good example. Lewis's "third world" of "romantic imagination" has a dominant role to play in this story from 1800 BCE. It is a fantasy that is a free myth for the purpose of entertainment. Lewis's "third world" existed and was alive and well some 3200 years before his "Renaissance."[4]

Loren R. Fisher
Walnut Creek, California
May 2009

4. Gopnik quotes from C. S. Lewis, *The Allegory of Love*, 82. Lewis in this book is difficult to read and hard to take. His Middle Ages are dark indeed, and then there is his "Renaissance." For a better understanding of the gradual growth of literature from ancient times and throughout the years from 600 to 1650 CE, one needs to read again Henry Osborn Taylor, *The Mediaeval Mind*, volumes 1 and 2. (C. S. Lewis fails to credit H. O. Taylor for his help on the subject of allegory.) This long period was not a period of birth and rebirth, but rather it was a period of continuation and discovery. There was enough freedom to allow the evolution of literature and other humanistic concerns to flower. The Greeks were well aware of what they inherited from the Egyptians. This is clear from Plato's *Phaedrus* (the discovery of writing) and *Timaeus,* and the traditions concerning Pythagoras are also helpful (see Burkert, *Lore and Science in Ancient Pythagoreanism*).

Acknowledgments

My teacher, Cyrus H. Gordon, wanted his students of ancient Mediterranean literature to work with all available texts. I have spent most of my time on Hebrew, Babylonian, and Ugaritic texts, but as I turn to Egyptian texts, I can only say, "I wish that I had done this earlier." Egyptian is such a delight. William A. Ward, one of my classmates, knew this from the start, and he was a great help to me during our student days and even during his years in Beirut.

I want to thank my son, John Fisher, for his painting for the cover of this book and for his illustration of "The Man and His Ba" in chapter 5. He has captured the Egyptian idea that the *Ba* is exactly like the Man. I thank Stan Rummel for his sharp eye and his willingness to share his vast knowledge of the humanities. I thank my wife, Jane Sheldon, for her editorial work. And I also thank my editor at Cascade Books, K. C. Hanson; he has prepared the indexes, and he has helped to improve this work with his many suggestions resulting from his careful reading and his knowledge of the Mediterranean world.

Abbreviations

AnOr	Analecta Orientalia
BHS	*Biblia Hebraica Stuttgartensia*
EA	Tel el-Amarna Letters
LXX	The Septuagint
MT	The Masoretic Text
NRSV	New Revised Standard Version of the Bible
RS	Ras Shamra text
RSP	*Ras Shamra Parallels*, edited by Loren R. Fisher and Stan Rummel
RSV	Revised Standard Version of the Bible
UL	Cyrus H. Gordon, *Ugaritic Literature: A Comprehensive Translation of the Poetic and Prose Texts*
UT	Cyrus H. Gordon, *Ugaritic Textbook*

Introduction

Unlike some other ancient states, both Israel and Egypt wrote epic tales in prose.[1] This prose, with a scattering of poetry, is not only important for our understanding of Israel and Egypt, but it is also important for a clear understanding of the history of world literature. Miriam Lichtheim, whose Egyptian translations have been praised, understood this. She wrote that "The Story of Sinuhe" "is the crown jewel of Middle Kingdom literature."[2] According to Lichtheim, the tomb is the setting for such a jewel; it is at the tomb that autobiography was born and true narrative literature took its shape.[3] I have referred to Lichtheim in my book *Genesis, A Royal Epic*, where I discuss the probability that the patriarchal narratives were also based on stories prepared for the tomb.[4]

1. Rendsburg, "The Genesis of the Bible," 27.

2. Lichtheim, *Ancient Egyptian Literature*, 1:11.

3. Autobiographies are important. They are in part fictional but filled with observable and actual facts. It is of some interest to relate these autobiographies with their detailed experiences to the thought of Charles Hartshorne in his *Omnipotence and Other Theological Mistakes*, 34–36. He says, "What is indeed immortal (the reality of the past) is precisely this infinite series of experiences and deeds."

4. Fisher, *Genesis, A Royal Epic*, 22.

For many years, I tended to focus on other aspects of ancient Mediterranean literature, but in my recent books, I have become serious about relating Egyptian texts to the growth of Hebrew tradition.[5] There are many interesting parallels, both great and small, between Hebrew and Egyptian prose tales. The details may vary, but in the setting, the purpose, the vocabulary, and the genre of the stories, one can find many similarities. Many scholars and students are not familiar with this literature, and therefore it is difficult for them to imagine what an important influence the Egyptians had in the east Mediterranean world. It may be even more difficult to imagine the impact that others had on the Egyptians, but it will become apparent from our discussion of these stories that this is the case.

The Egyptian story "The Eloquent Peasant" was popular during the Middle Kingdom and is extremely important to any discussion of new insights and contributions to civilization. But I did not include that story in this book because I would like to devote a separate book to it. That story captures what John Wilson describes as a "sublime vision" of individual and social justice,[6] but the "vision" was blurred by the growth of the empire. Sadly, this chain of events is familiar to us again today. The forced growth of the United States of America Empire from 2001 through 2008 again blurred our vision of individual and social justice.

The story "The Enchanted Prince" was written later than "Sinuhe" or "The Eloquent Peasant"—about six hun-

5. Ibid.; see also, Fisher, *The Jerusalem Academy*; and Fisher, *The Minority Report*.

6. Wilson, *The Culture of Ancient Egypt*, 124.

dred years later, or around 1400 BCE. It introduced the fairytale theme that we know today in the many Rapunzel tales, but it also helps us to understand historical developments of this period. The setting of the story in northern Mesopotamia informs us of the impact of Egypt on its world, and in this case the Hurrian influence on the Egyptians.[7]

The third story in this book, "The Story of the Shipwrecked Sailor," was written earlier, in 1800 BCE. It probably circulated for many years in an oral form; it was an entertaining story. You will discover that it is the first of an exciting genre of shipwreck stories, complete with enchanted islands and fascinating experiences.

About a thousand years after "The Story of Sinuhe" first appeared, "The Journey of Wen-Amon" was written during the last part of the reign of Ramses XI, about 1090 to 1080 BCE. I take the position, along with many others, that this story or report concerns a real journey. In any case, it tells us a great deal about Egypt and Phoenicia at this time. The ending to Wen-Amon's report is missing, but the fact that we have the report is usually taken as proof that Wen-Amon did return to Egypt and wrote this account of his travels.

Finally, I have included "A Dialogue between a Man and His *Ba*" because it is a great witness to the kinds of problems that humans have always faced. This story is especially important for me because of my intensive studies of the book of Job. Both employ the same structure of prose plus poetry plus prose, and this cannot be overlooked. In

7. For more details, see the introduction to chapter 2 and the conclusion of this volume.

Egyptian *Ba* can usually be translated as "soul." In Hebrew I usually translate *nephesh* not as "soul" but as "being," but in Job, because of this man and his *Ba*, I have sometimes translated the Hebrew as "soul." Note Job 10:1:

> My soul is disgusted with my life;
> > I will give free rein to my complaint;
> > I will speak from the bitterness of my soul.

For all of these stories, I have received help from many translated examples in Sir Alan Gardiner's *Egyptian Grammar*, from Adolf Erman and Hermann Grapow's *Wörterbuch der Aegyptischen Sprache*, and the translations of others.

1

The Story of Sinuhe:
A Wanderer on Earth

Introduction

"The Story of Sinuhe" comes to us from the Twelfth Dynasty, about 1960 BCE. This beautiful story followed the style of the older autobiographies of Weni and Harkhuf from the Sixth Dynasty, about 2300–2150 BCE. But "The Story of Sinuhe" surpassed all earlier examples.

This story is extremely important for our under-standing of epic literature in Egypt and in Israel. Unlike the poetic epics of Greece and Ugarit, epic tales in Egypt and Israel were written in prose with a few poems scattered throughout. Miriam Lichtheim has an interesting discus-sion of how in Egypt, "it was in the context of the private tomb that writing took its first steps toward literature."[1] I repeat these comments for the purpose of pointing out that my suggestions in my earlier writings concerning the

1. Lichtheim, *Ancient Egyptian Literature*, 1:3–4.

growth of Hebrew literature at the tomb are not new in our studies of ancient literature. But it certainly may be new for many to think about the growth of the patriarchal cycles at the tomb.[2] The tomb was the place where the stories of the ancestors were told, sung, and written, and in the case of Egypt, perhaps stories were written on the tombs.

Miriam Lichtheim says that "The Story of Sinuhe" "is the crown jewel of Middle Kingdom literature"[3] Lichtheim's comment on "Sinuhe" reads: "Through its beginning and its ending, the story is given the form of the tomb-autobiography in which the narrator looks back on his completed life."[4] Besides Lichtheim, other translators have been helpful in this work including John Wilson,[5] William Simpson,[6] and A. F. Rainey.[7]

2. Fisher, *Genesis: A Royal Epic*, 22–25. Here you will find a detailed discussion of this with reference to Abraham, Isaac, and Jacob.

3. Lichtheim, *Ancient Egyptian Literature*, 1:11.

4. Ibid., 1:235 n. 26.

5. Wilson, "Sinuhe."

6. Simpson, "Sinuhe."

7. Rainey, "The World of Sinuhe."

The Story of Sinuhe[8]

(R 1) <u>The Prince,</u>[9] ruler, and honorable administrator of the estates of the sovereign in the lands of the Asiatics,[10] a Friend of the king,[11] his love was true, the orderly Sinuhe, he says:

I was an attendant who followed his lord, a servant of the king's harem, of the princess, who was greatly praised, the wife of King Sesostris in Khenemsut,[12] the daughter of King Amenemhet (R 5) in Qanefru,[13] Nefru, the Great Lady.[14]

<u>Year 30, month 3 of the inundation, day 7</u>: the god[15] ascended to his horizon, the King of Upper and Lower

---

8. The hieroglyphic text for this translation is found in Blackman, *Middle-Egyptian Stories,* 1–41. The two best texts are Berlin 3022 (B) and Berlin 10499 (R). The beginning of B is lost, so we begin with R. I will note the text and the line number every five lines. There are other texts as well. At the end of the story, Text L is helpful.

9. Where the text has a section or word underlined, I have done the same. The scribe has underlined important words, phrases, and titles of documents.

10. Several peoples and/or countries are designated "Asiatics," who were situated in Palestine and Syria. It seems that Sinuhe is claiming that he ruled in this country for Egypt.

11. This is a technical term; he is close to the king and an officer in the king's administration.

12. This was his pyramid city.

13. This was his pyramid city.

14. A title. Note *ra-bi-ti*, "The Great Lady" in Text RS 1957.1 from Ugarit. See Fisher, *The Claremont Ras Shamra Texts*, 11–21. The "Great Lady" (or "queen mother," *gebirah*) is also mentioned in the Hebrew Bible: 1 Kings 11:19; 15:12; and 2 Kings 10:13.

15. This is the king.

Egypt, Sehetep-ib-re.[16] He flew up to the sky and was joined with the sun disk; the god's flesh was united with that of his Maker.[17]

Then the residence[18] was in silence:

Hearts were in mourning.
  The great double gates were sealed. (R 10)
  The courtiers were with head on lap.
  All humans were in mourning.

Now his majesty had sent an army to the land of Temeh;[19] his eldest son was the commander, the good god Sesostris. He had been sent to strike the foreign lands and to subdue those among the Tehenu.[20] (R 15) But now he was returning, and he was bringing prisoners of the Tehenu and an endless (line) of cattle of all kinds. The courtiers of the palace sent (a message) to the western border to make known to the king's son what had happened at the court. The messengers found him on the road; (R 20) they reached him in the late evening. Not a moment at all did he delay. The Falcon[21] flew with his followers, not making it known to the army. Also the royal sons, who were with him in this army, had been sent for. (B 1) One of them was summoned, and while I was standing there, I heard (the

16. The Prenomen (one of the five names of kings) of Amenemhet.

17. This reports the death of Amenemhet I about 1960 BCE, and now Sesostris I, his son and coregent, will become king.

18. This is the capital city, which contains the palace.

19. Where the Libyans lived, west of Egypt.

20. Another group of Libyans. This sentence is only in the R text and is left out in Wilson, "Sinuhe," 18.

21. This is Sesostris, the new king.

messenger's)²² voice as he was speaking. I was nearby. My heart²³ was distraught, my arms opened wide, and trembling fell upon all my limbs. I removed myself, leaping to find a hiding place. I put (B 5) myself between two bushes in order to free the road for its travelers.

I set out to go to the south. I did not plan to approach the residence. I thought there would be a civil war and did not think there would be life after it. I crossed Ma'aty near Sycamore, and I reached the Island of Snefru. I spent the day at the edge (B 10) of the cultivated land. I set out early the next day. I met a man who was standing on the road. He showed respect for me; he was fearful. When the time of the evening meal came, I reached the town of Nagau. I crossed over²⁴ in a barge, which had no rudder, with a west wind. I passed to the east of the quarry, (B 15) above the Goddess of the Red Mountain. I set my feet on the road going north,²⁵ and I arrived at the Walls of the Prince, which was made to repel the Asiatics and to crush the Sand-farers.²⁶ I crouched in a bush for fear that the watchmen upon the wall might see me during their watch. I departed (B 20) at night, and by morning

22. The text has "his voice."

23. As in Hebrew, the word for "heart" can also refer to the mind. This could involve both. His mind was also troubled. We are not told why he was so frightened, but regime change is always a dangerous time.

24. Here he crossed the Nile.

25. It is interesting to compare "I set my feet" to Genesis 29:1 and the flight and travels of Jacob. The verse reads: "Jacob lifted his feet; he went to the land of the Bene-Qedem" or the sons of Qedem (or: "Jacob directed his feet to the land of the Bene-Qedem.").

26. This last phrase is from Text R.

I reached Peten. I stopped at the Island of Kem-wer (the Great Black). Thirst quickly fell upon me. I was parched; my throat was hot. I said, "This is the taste of death." But then I strengthened my heart and collected myself for I heard the lowing of (B 25) cattle, and I saw Asiatics. Their leader, one who had been in Egypt, recognized me; he gave me water and boiled milk for me. I accompanied him to his tribe; they treated me well.

Land gave me to land. I departed to Byblos, and I returned to Qedem.[27] I spent (B 30) a year and a half there. Ammi-enshi, who was the ruler of Upper Retenu,[28] took me, and he said to me, "You will be happy with me; you will hear the language of Egypt." He said this because he knew of my character. He had heard of my wisdom. The people of Egypt, who were there with him, gave witness to me.

Then he said to me, "Why (B 35) have you come here? What has caused this? Has something happened in the palace?"[29]

27. See Job 1:3, where Job is greater than the Bene-Qedem.

28. This refers to central and northern Syria. Here we have "the ruler of Upper Retenu," but the more usual Egyptian phrase is "ruler of a foreign land," and that became the basis from the Egyptian for our terminology "Hyksos." Rainey, "The World of Sinuhe," 374, says, "There is no justification whatever for placing the 'Hyksos' alongside of the Hurrians, the 'Apiru, to name a few, as another ethic element in the Levantine population. The 'Hyksos' were city-state rulers before they invaded Egypt, and they continued to rule Levantine city-states after their expulsion."

29. These questions by his host are like the serpent's questions to the shipwrecked sailor ("Who brought you to this island?").

Then I said to him,[30] "The King of Upper and Lower
Egypt, Sehetep-ib-re, has departed to the horizon. No one
knows what will happen because of it." I spoke with some
deception. "I had come from an expedition to the Land of
Temeh when it was reported to me.

> My mind was blurred.
> My heart, it was not in my body.[31]
> It carried (B 40) me off on the way of flight.
> No one gossiped about me.
> No one spat in my face.
> No reproach was heard.
> My name was not heard from the mouth of a herald.
> I do not know what brought me to this country.
> It was as if planned by a god."[32]

Then he said,[33] "What will the land be like without
him, that excellent god, the fear[34] of whom was through-

30. This phrase is from R 59.

31. This phrase is in Text B and misspelled; it is not in the other
texts. Simpson, "Sinuhe," 61, uses it, but others leave it out. Gardiner,
Egyptian Grammar, 92, example 3, says that the text is corrupt but
gives the correct form as used in B 255. I follow Simpson because it
works well with the next line. This same poem is repeated in B 224
to B 230 but in a longer form.

32. This is similar to the Joseph story in the Hebrew Bible. In
Genesis 45:5 Joseph says to his brothers, "Elohim sent me ahead of
you." Or note Genesis 50:20, "You planned evil against me. Elohim
planned it for good . . . " At this point Lichtheim, *Ancient Egyptian
Literature,* vol. 1, inserts R 65–67, "As if a Delta-man saw himself in
Yebu, a marsh-man in Nubia." Or see Gardiner, *Egyptian Grammar,*
357, example 11, "As when a man of the marshes sees himself in
Elephantine."

33. This phrase is from R. Ammi-enshi is still speaking.

34. "Fear" is required for gods or kings. It insures that their
people or slaves are obedient.

out (B 45) the foreign lands like that of Sakhmet in a year of plague?"

I spoke to him; I gave him an answer, "Certainly his son has entered the palace. He has received the inheritance of his father:

> He is a god who has no equal.
> No other will surpass him.[35]
> He is the lord of wisdom.
> He is an excellent planner.
> He is an extraordinary commander.
> Going forth and returning are by his (B 50) command.
> He subdued foreign lands.
> While his father was in his palace,
> He reported to him on orders completed.
> He is a hero who conquers with his mighty arm.
> He is a champion.
> There is none like him,
> When seen charging the bowmen
> Or attacking the unjust.
> This is the one who bends the horn.[36]
> He makes hands weak.
> His enemies (B 55) cannot form ranks.
> With anger, skulls are crushed.
> No one stands near him.
> With great strides he strikes those who flee.
> There is no escape for the one who turns his back to him.
> He is strong of heart at the time of striking the back.

35. Such a claim can be seen in Psalm 89:7: "For who in the skies will equal Yahweh or will compare with Yahweh among the *bene-'elim* (sons of the gods or divine beings)?" This hymn of praise for Seostris I is a bit much.

36. "Horn" means, "bow."

He is one who comes again.

He does not turn his back.

He is stout of heart when he sees a crowd.

He does not allow cowardice in his heart.

(B 60) He is courageous when he sees the enemy.

He enjoys it when he attacks the archers.

Taking his shield, he crushes.

He does not need to stomp again to kill.

There is none who can dodge his arrow.

No one can stretch his bow.

The bowmen flee before him,

Like from the might of a goddess.

As he fights he plans the goal.

(B 65) He does not protect himself and certainly not
the remnants,

But he is complete with favor and extremely kind.

He conquers with love.

His city loves him more than itself.

They rejoice in him more than their God.

Men and women are jubilant with him as they pass by,

Now that he is king.

He conquered while still in the egg.

He was determined since he was born.

He has multiplied those who were born with him.

(B 70) He is one who is given by God.

Joyful is this land, which he rules.

He has enlarged its boundaries.

He will seize the southern lands.

He was made to smite the Asiatics

And tread on the Sand-farers.[37]

---

37. These are the Bedouin.

Send to him (a message)! Let him know your name, as one who inquires though far from his majesty. He will not fail to do (B 75) good to a country that is loyal to him."

He said to me, "Indeed, Egypt is happy knowing that she is strong. But you are here; you will be with me. What I shall do for you is good."

He placed me at the head of his children. He married me to his eldest daughter.[38] He allowed me to choose for myself from his country, (B 80) from the choicest of that which was his, on the border with another country. This land was beautiful; its name was Yaa.[39] There were figs in it and vineyards. It had more wine than water. Its honey was abundant and plentiful its olive oil. Every kind of fruit was on its trees. There was barley along with emmer. All the cattle herds were without number. (B 85) Moreover, great gifts were brought to me; they came because of the love of me. He made me chief of a tribe from the best part of his country. Bread was served to me daily (plus) a fine wine, cooked meat, roast fowl, besides the wild beasts of the dessert. (B 90) For they used to snare for me and would bring it for me, in addition to what my hounds caught. They made many things for me, and all were boiled in milk.[40]

38. This is the usual practice as seen in the story of Jacob in Genesis 29:26, where Laban gave Leah to Jacob.

39. The practice of making land grants to worthy subjects is well known in the Levant, and is well known at Ugarit at a much later time. In the Hebrew Bible, Achish grants the town of Ziklag to David (1 Samuel 27:5–6); David grants Saul's lands to Meribaal (2 Samuel 9:1–13); Absalom and Joab's fields presuppose royal land grants (2 Samuel 14:30–31); and Pharaoh grants Hadad of Edom a house, land, and food allowance (1 Kings 11:18).

40. Hence not kosher for the later Hebrews.

I spent many years, and (from) my children came strong men, each a chief of his tribe. The messenger who came north or went south to the palace (B 95) stayed with me. I invited everyone to stay with me.[41] I gave water to the thirsty. I put the one who strayed back on the road. I rescued him who had been robbed. When the Asiatics became aggressive, in order to dominate the rulers of foreign countries, I opposed their actions. This ruler of (B 100) Retenu appointed me to spend many years as the commander of his army. Every foreign country against which I marched, I attacked, and it was driven from its pasture and its wells. I took its cattle and captured its families. I seized their food, and I killed people by (B 105) my mighty arm, by my bow, by my maneuvers, and by my excellent plans. This seemed good in his heart; he loved me. He knew I was brave. He placed me at the head of his children, when he saw the strength of my arms.

> Then came a hero of Retenu,
> To challenge me (B 110) in my own camp.
> He was a champion, this one, without equal.
> He had subdued all of it.
> He said he would fight with me.
> He intended to rob me.
> He planned to take my cattle,
> On the counsel of his tribe.

That ruler discussed this with me. I said, I do not know him; I am not his confederate (B 115) that I could walk freely in his encampment. Is it the case that I have opened his cattle pens or that I have gone over his wall?

41. Simpson, "Sinuhe," 63, has a strange translation: "and I made all Egyptians stay."

This is envy, because he sees me doing his[42] assignment. Indeed, I am like a bull from a wandering herd in the midst of another herd (whose bull) attacks the bull of the wandering herd (B 120) of cattle, but (the stray bull)[43] is victorious against him. Is a poor man loved when he is appointed as a ruler over me?[44] No foreign bowman unites with a Delta-man. What would join a papyrus marsh with a mountain of stone? Does the bull want to fight? If so a champion bull will want to accept for fear of being equated with him. (B 125) If it is his wish to fight, let him say what is in his heart. Is there a god who does not know what he appointed, that is, knowing how it is?

During the night I strung my bow and shot my arrows. I laid out my daggers and polished my weapons. At dawn Retenu came (B 130), it incited its tribes and assembled half of the countries that had planned this fight.[45]

He came to me; I was waiting, having placed myself near him.[46] Every heart burned for me; women and men murmured. Every heart was sick for me. They said, "Is

42. Other translators change the "his" to "your." In one sense they are correct. The orders come from Sinuhe's ruler. But the text understands that Sinuhe now does what the "hero" was told to do. Sinuhe does the business of the "hero."

43. The text only has "he."

44. In Proverbs 30:22a, we are told that the earth shudders or quakes at "A slave who has become king."

45. This combat has been compared to the David and Goliath battle of champions. I do not agree with Hoffner, "A Hittite Analogue to the David and Goliath Contest," 220, where he calls the Sinuhe battle a personal duel and not a battle of champions. The battle of champions in the Sinhue story and the Hebrew Bible are discussed by de Vaux, *Ancient Israel*, 218; and Hertzberg, *I & II Samuel*, 148 n. b.

46. This sentence is from R 156.

there another hero who could fight against him? Then he raised his shield, his axe (B 135); and his armful of javelins were hurled toward me. I caused his weapons to pass by me. His arrows amounted to nothing, one after the other. Then he charged me, and I shot him. My arrow stuck in his neck. He cried out; he fell on his face.[47] (B 140). I slew him with his axe,[48] and I raised my war cry over his back. Every Asiatic shouted, and I gave praise to Montu.[49] His friends mourned him. This ruler, Ammi-enshi, took me into his arms. Then I removed his property, and I plundered his herds. He planned to do (B 145) it to me, but I did it to him. I seized what was in his tent; I plundered his camp. I became great, abundant in wealth, and my herds were many.[50] So god acted with mercy. He forgave the one

---

47. The story of David and Goliath (1 Samuel 17) and the story of Sinuhe both contain a scene depicting a battle of champions. There are several interesting parallels in these stories, but two are outstanding. In both, the enemy falls on his face. In Akkadian letters, the inferior person begins with obeisance or homage to the addressee. In an Amarna letter (EA 286) from the fourteenth century BCE, the ruler of Jerusalem, 'Abdi-Heba, says in a letter he sent to Egypt, "I fall at the feet of my lord, the king, seven times and seven times." In a battle of champions when the opponent falls on his face, he becomes a 'servant' to Sinuhe or to David, albeit in these cases dead servants. Also we note that in both stories the hero uses the opponent's weapon to kill him, and in David's case to cut off his head. Note also the battles of champions in the *Iliad*: Paris and Menalaus (*Iliad* 3) and Hector and Ajax (*Iliad* 7); see Gordon, "Homer and the Bible," 87.

48. It is difficult to understand why Simpson translates "my axe."

49. Montu was the Egyptian god of war.

50. In the stories of the patriarchs either the father or his wife is endangered, but in the end there is success and great wealth.

whom he had caused to wander to another country. Today his heart is appeased.

(Then and Now)[51]

A fugitive fled (B 150) his environs.
  I am renowned at the palace.
A wanderer staggered with hunger.
  I give bread to my neighbor.
A man departed his land naked.
  I have bright clothes of fine linen.
A man ran for lack of a messenger.
  I am (B 155) one rich in servants.
  My house is beautiful.
  My domain is large.
  They remember me at the palace.

Whoever from all the gods commanded this flight, be forgiving and restore me to the palace. Surely you will grant me to see where my heart dwells. What is a greater thing than that my body should be buried in the land in

---

51. I have added this title for the following poem. It is not in the text. Also I would also like to quote the translation of this poem by Gordon in *Before the Bible*, 106–7. His "Once" and "Now" are not in the text, but the text does alternate between past and present:

Once a fugitive fled
  Now there are reports of me in the palace.
Once a straggler dragged along, a victim of hunger
  Now I give bread to my neighbor.
Once a man left his land because of misfortune
  Now I shine in robes of linen.
Once a man ran, for want of anyone to send
  Now I'm rich in slaves.
  My house is beautiful; my domain is large.
  They mention me in the palace.

which I was born?[52] (B 160) Come, after this happy occasion. May god give me rest. May he act now so as to make things excellent in the end, for he has shown his anger. His heart was bitter because of the one whom he expelled to live in a foreign country. Is it the case today that he is forgiving? May he hear the prayer of one far away. May he bring back the one whom he caused to wander the earth from his presence to the place from which he exiled him.

May (B 165) the King of Egypt have mercy on me; I live by his mercies. May I inquire concerning the needs of the mistress of the land, who is in his palace. May I respond to the requests of her children. Would that my body were young again. But old age descended upon it. Misery has overtaken me; my eyes are weak. (B 170) My legs, they fail to serve; the heart is weary. Near to me is my passing. They shall conduct me to the eternal cities. I shall serve the Mistress of All. May she speak well of me to her children. May she pass eternity above me.[53]

Now when his majesty, the King of Upper and Lower Egypt, Kheperkare,[54] the justified,[55] was told concerning this state in which I was, thereupon his majesty sent

52. In most of these stories, the homecoming theme is basic. Note Jacob's desire for his body to be returned to Canaan for burial with his kin (Genesis 49:29–32).

53. Simpson, "Sinuhe," 66 n. 14, makes an interesting point: "It seems that the queen is here identified with the sky goddess; her image, surrounded with stars, is generally placed on the underside of the coffin or sarcophagus lid above the body."

54. Another name for Sesostris.

55. This justification is literally "just/true of voice" that is usually achieved after death in the burial ritual, but sometimes kings are declared "true of voice" before death. See Montet, *Everyday Life in Egypt*, 306.

(B 175) presents to me with which he made joyful the heart of this servant like the ruler of a foreign land. The royal children, who were in his palace, made known their messages.

Copy of the decree, which was brought to this servant concerning his return to Egypt: "Horus, Living in Births;[56] Two Ladies, Living in Births; the King of Upper and Lower Egypt: Kheperkare; the Son of Re: (B 180) Sesostris, who lives forever. The king's command to the Attendant Sinuhe:

"Behold, this decree of the king is brought to you to let you know that indeed you went around foreign lands, going from Qedem to Retenu. Land gave you to Land. [But this was] under the counsel of your heart to you. What had you done that one should act against you? You had not cursed so that your words should be repressed. You had not spoken against the counsel of the nobles that your sayings should be opposed. (B 185) This plan carried away your heart; nothing was in (any) heart against you. This, your 'heaven,'[57] who is in the palace, is well and flourishes today. Her head is covered with royalty of the land. Her children are in the palace.

"You shall keep the riches which they give you; you shall live on their bounty.

56. In Excursus A ("The Titulary and other Designations of the King"), Gardiner provides a detailed discussion of a king's five names (*Egyptian Grammar*, 71–76). The first Horus name is followed by "Living in Births" as is the second name. Gardiner translates "Life-of-births." The meaning of this is difficult, but it may mean that Horus lives again each time a king is born.

57. Here "heaven" refers to the queen.

"Return to Egypt! You will see the residence where you were born. In it you will kiss the ground at the great double gates, and you will join with the courtiers. Today, surely, you (B 190) have begun to grow old. You have left behind masculine strength. Think concerning the day of burial, the passing to an honored state, and the night will be reserved for you with ointments and wrappings from the hands of Tait.[58] A funeral procession will be made for you on the day of burial; the mummy case will be of gold, its head of lapis lazuli. Heaven will be over you; you will be placed on the sledge. Oxen will drag you with musicians leading. The dance of the (B 195) *mww*-dancers will be performed at the door of the tomb. The full menu of offerings will be called forth for you; sacrifice will be made before your stone altar.[59] Tomb pillars will be carved from white stone in the midst of (those of) the royal children. You shall not die in a foreign land. Asiatics shall not escort you. You shall not be placed in a sheep hide when they make your tomb. This has been too long for a wanderer on earth. Care for the corpse. Return!"

This decree reached me as I stood in the (B 200) midst of my people.

58. The goddess of weaving.

59. The cult of the dead is important for most of our studies. For a detailed discussion of the cult of the dead in the Mediterranean world and especially for the origin of Egyptian and Hebrew cults, see Fisher, *Genesis, A Royal Epic*, 22–30; this is also developed in detail in Fisher, *The Jerusalem Academy* and *The Minority Report*. I have also discussed some of these matters in the introduction to this book. For stone altars note Jacob setting up a pillar at Rachel's grave (Genesis 35:19–20); or Absalom setting up his own memorial pillar (2 Samuel 18:18).

It was read to me. I prostrated myself on my belly. I touched the soil; I scattered it on my hair. I went around my camp rejoicing and saying: "How can this be done for a servant whom his heart led astray to foreign lands? Indeed it is good, the forgiveness, which has saved me from death. Your *Ka*[60] will allow me to reach my goal; my body will be in the residence."

A copy of the answer to this decree. The servant of the palace, Sinuhe, (B 205) says with good and great peace: "This flight, which this servant made in ignorance, is known by your Ka, O good God, Lord of the Two Lands, whom Re loves and whom Montu, Lord of Thebes, praises, and Amun, Lord of the Thrones of the Two Lands, and Sobk-Re,[61] Horus, Hathor. Atum with the Ennead, Sopdu, Neferbau, Semseru, Horus of the East, the Lady Yemet, may she join your head of the council on the flood, Min-Horus in the midst if the hill country, Wereret, Lady (B 210) of Punt, Nut, Haroeris-Re, and all the gods of the beloved land[62] and the islands of the Great Green.[63] May they give life and success to your nostrils. May they endow you with gifts. May they give you everlastingness without end and eternity without limit. May the fear of you echo throughout the flatlands and the hill country. You have subdued all that the sun disk surrounds."

---

60. *Ka* is used to indicate spirit/soul.

61. Others insert here "Lord of Sumenu."

62. The phrase "the beloved land" refers to Egypt.

63. The phrase "Great Green" can refer to both the Mediterranean and the Red Sea.

This is the prayer of this servant for his Lord, who saves from the West.[64] "Lord of knowledge, who knows common folks, he knows (B 215) in the majesty of the palace that this servant was afraid to say it.[65] It is like something too big to repeat. The great God, an equal of Re, knows a servant, who gives of himself. This servant has been given to one who asks about him. He is placed under his plan. Your majesty is the victorious Horus; your two arms are over all lands.

"May your majesty command that there be brought out Maki from Qedem, (B 220) from among the rebels of the prison of Keshu, and Menus from the lands of the Fenkhu.[66] They are rulers with worthy names, who have grown up loving you. Not to mention the Retenu, who belong to you just like your hounds.

Now, this flight, which your servant made:

> I did not plan it.
> It was not in my heart.
> I did not devise it.[67]
> I do not know what separated me from (my) place.

64. He saves or rescues from the West or from death. "West" is a metaphor of death because the burial hill was located west of the Nile.

65. In "The Story of the Shipwrecked Sailor," the sailor is also afraid to speak.

66. This is a difficult line. No one else translates it this way. I do not think the other translations are correct, and I am not certain of mine. The word "rebel" perhaps should be a *Nekhi'wš* rebel (note the determinative). For "prison" see Gardiner, *Egyptian Grammar*, 201 n. 1.

67. Notice the short and staccato sentences. Such sentences have been run together by most translators of Genesis 38:1–9. This poem is a repeat of B 39–B 43, but it has been expanded.

It was like (B 225) following a dream.
(As if a man of the marshes sees himself in
   Elephantine,
or a man of the marsh in Nubia.)[68]
I was not afraid.
No one had run after me.
I did not hear an abusive word.
My name was not heard from the mouth of herald.
But my body shivered.
My feet were running.
My heart moved me.
The god who commanded this flight (B 230) drew
   me on.

I am not arrogant. In the presence of fear, a man learns about his land. Re has put the fear of you throughout the land and the dread of you in every foreign country. Whether I am at the residence or whether I am in this place, you are the one who covers this horizon. The sun disk rises at your pleasure. The water in the river is drunk when you wish. The air of the heavens is breathed when you say so. This servant will bequeath (B 235) (all) to my children, whom this servant has brought up in this place. This servant has been recalled. Your majesty will do as he wants. One lives by the air that you give. Re, Horus, and Hathor love your noble nose. (Also) beloved by Montu, Lord of Thebes, may it live.

I was allowed to pass a day in Yaa to hand over my property to my children. My eldest son took charge of my

68. See above n. 32. This sentence is also found in R 65–67 and was inserted in the middle of B 43 in Lichtheim, *Ancient Egyptian Literature*, 1:225. Here it is in the text, but it seems to interrupt the poem. I put it in parentheses.

tribe. (B 240) My tribe and all my things were in his hands: my serfs, all my cattle, my fruit, and all my date trees.

This your servant departed to the south. I stopped at the Ways of Horus.[69] The commander, who was in charge of the border guards, sent a message to the residence to make them aware. Then his majesty sent an able overseer of the peasants of the palace along with loaded ships (B 245) carrying royal gifts for the Asiatics, who had come with me, to escort me to the Ways of Horus. I called everyone there by his name. Every butler was at work. When I started and set sail, kneading (dough in water) and straining (it for beer) was done beside me until I reached the town of 'Itw.[70]

When it dawned and it was morning, they came and summoned me; ten men came, and ten men went back, conducting me to the palace.[71] My forehead touched the ground between the sphinxes, (B 250) and the royal children stood in the gateway in order to greet me. Then courtiers came into the reception-hall to set me on the way to the inner audience chamber. I found his majesty on the great throne in a recess of fine gold. Now I was stretched out on my belly; I did not know myself in his presence. This god addressed me in a friendly manner. I was like a man overtaken by darkness. (B 255) My soul

69. An Egyptian frontier station.

70. For a detailed account of how the Egyptians made beer from bread and water, see Homan, "Beer and Its Drinkers: An Ancient Near Eastern Love Story."

71. It is interesting that in an apparently later text (OP2) the word for palace is a different word, and it is followed by the later tradition of adding the abbreviations for "life," "prosperity," and "health."

departed; my flesh became weak. My heart was not in my body that I might know life from death.

Then his majesty said to one of these courtiers: "Lift him up. Let him speak to me." Then his majesty said, "Now you have returned. You have wandered in foreign lands. This flight has caused loss. You are old; you have reached old age. Your corpse is not a small matter. You shall not be interred by Asiatics. Do not, do not act this way. You do not speak (B 260) when your name is pronounced."

Indeed, I was afraid of punishment. I answered this with an answer from my frightened self. "What is it that my lord has said to me? I should answer it, but I cannot do it. Indeed, this is the hand of god. Dread exists in my body like that, which caused my fated flight. Here I am in your presence. Life is yours. May your majesty do as he pleases."[72]

Then the king's daughters were brought in, and his majesty said to his queen, "Here is Sinuhe, (B 265) who has returned as an Asiatic, created by the Bedouin."

She made a great cry, and the king's daughters shrieked together. Then they said in the presence of his majesty, "In truth it is not he, O king, our[73] lord."

Then his majesty said, "In truth it is he."

Now they brought their bead necklaces, their rattles, and their sistra; they presented them to his majesty:

72. This paragraph is similar to the passage in "The Story of the Shipwrecked Sailor" where the sailor is afraid to answer the serpent. To speak up and not be afraid becomes the major theme in the story.

73. "Our" and not "my" as in Simpson, "Sinuhe,"72; and Wilson, "Sinuhe," 22.

Your arms[74] are for (B 270) good, O king eternal.
(These are) ornaments of the Lady of Heaven.
The Golden One gives life to your nostrils.[75]
The Lady of the Stars is joined (with you).

The crown of Upper Egypt went north.
The crown of Lower Egypt went south.
Joined and brought together by the word of your
majesty.
The Cobra Goddess has been put on your brow.

You have kept the poor from harm.
Peace to you from Re, Lord of the Two Lands.
Hail to you and to the Mistress of All.
Unstring your bow; unloose your arrow (B 275).

Give breath to him who is breathless.
Grant us our good gift.
This is a Bedouin hunter, son of the North Wind.
He is a bowman born in Egypt.

He made the flight from fear of you.
He departed the land through dread of you.
The face will not pale that sees your face.
The eye will not fear that looks at you.

His majesty said, "He shall not fear; (B 280) he shall
not be given to dread. He shall be a Friend among the
nobles; he shall be placed in the midst of the courtiers.

74. His "arms" or "hand" could also refer to his "power."
75. The "Golden One" is Hathor.

Proceed to the morning-preparation room to prepare (him) for his position."[76]

I left the audience hall. The king's daughters gave me their hands. (B 285) We departed through the great double doors. I was put in the house of a royal son. Riches were in it: a cool room was in it, images of the horizon, valuables in it belonging to the treasury, clothing of royal linen, myrrh, and choice quality oil of the king and the nobles whom he loves were in every room. (B 290) Every butler was about his work. Years were removed from my body. I was cleaned up; my hair was combed. Then the clothing was returned to the land of the sand dwellers. I was dressed in fine linen; I was anointed with top quality oil; I passed the night on a bed; I gave the sand to those who are on it (B 295), tree oil to those who are anointed with it. I was given the house of a lord with its garden, which had belonged to a courtier.[77] Many craftsmen worked on it, and all of its wood was made strong. Meals were brought to me from the palace, three times even four times in a day, in addition to that which the king's children gave, never ceasing for a moment. (B 300)

A pyramid of stone was built for me in the midst of the pyramids. The overseer of the masons also made its floor plan. The master draftsman wrote in it. The master sculptor carved in it.[78] The overseer of the workers, who was in the tomb, was attentive. All the equipment, which

76. Sinuhe is prepared here and even more so in lines B 290–93. The scene is like that in the story of Joseph in Genesis 41:14 and 42. Plus they are both dressed in fine linen.

77. In royal grants, the house and garden are usually listed.

78. For some of this, I have been helped by looking at Text L.

is placed in a tomb-shaft, (B305) was supplied. Ka-priests were given to me. There was made for me a garden tomb with its fields extending to town like that which is done for a chief courtier. My statue was overlaid with gold and its apron with fine gold. Indeed, it was his majesty who had it made. There was never a poor man for whom the like has ever been done. I was under (B 310) the favor of the king until the coming of the day of mooring.[79]

It has come, from its beginning to its end, like it was found in writing.

---

79. Here the determinatives after "mooring" are two: the mooring post and the sign for death.

Best wishes and tokens of respect as abbreviated by Egyptian scribes.

$^{c}n\underline{h}$ 　　 $w\underline{d}$? 　　 snb

Life 　　 Prosperity 　　 Health

2

The Enchanted Prince

Nuzi lay buried for centuries; the excavation of Nuzi began in 1925 under the direction of Edward Chiera. The Iraq Museum and the American School of Oriental Research in Baghdad sponsored it. In 1927 Harvard University replaced the Iraq Museum as a joint sponsor. Nuzi is about ten miles southwest of modern Kirkuk. We now know that the city of Kirkuk is the center of oil production in northeast Iraq, and it is also an important population and cultural center for the Kurds.[1]

Kirkuk was also an important center in the ancient history of northern Iraq or Mesopotamia. In ancient times, Kirkuk was known as Arrapha; it was also called "The City of the Gods (*al Ilâni*). In 1500 BCE Arrapha was an important city of the Mitanni Kingdom, or Hanigalbat

1. In their stories the Kurds reveal many ancient traditions. These traditions are not only pre-Islamic but some of them deal with social customs that we know from the Nuzi tablets. At Nuzi there are many adoption texts. In the story of "Sultan Mahmood and Heyas," the miller and his wife make Heyas an offer. She says, "We do not have a son, and we would like you to be our son. Do you agree?" For these Kurdish stories, see Edgecomb, *A Fire in My Heart*.

as it was called in the texts from Nuzi. The Mitanni Kingdom ran west as far as the Mediterranean, with the Hurrians forming the major part of the population. They were Indo-Europeans as were the Hittites, who populated what we know today as Turkey. The Egyptians called this area Naharin, and they called Syria "Khor," from the name of the Hurrian population.

In the Egyptian "Story of Sinuhe" from about 1960 BCE, we see early contacts with the people of Naharin. This story shows us that an Egyptian like Sinuhe was treated with great respect. "The Enchanted Prince" was written in about 1400 BCE. This story is much later, but it also has the prince going to Naharin. The storyteller places the action in the north in the Mitanni Kingdom, and for this reason, I have assumed that the story took place in or near Nuzi or Arrapha. I could not prove this; it was a possibility. I still cannot prove it, but now it is much more than a possibility.

In this story the Egyptian goddess Hathor (or her goddesses), gives the prince his Fates. In fact, the entire story deals with the Fates. When the prince married the princess, she was not only a confident and efficient woman, but she also seemed to know what to do about the Fates. How can we account for this? While musing on these questions, I made a discovery, which I should have uncovered years ago. The reports of the Nuzi excavation contains detailed drawings and plates,[2] and Richard Starr has made some interesting comments about the palace and the beautiful wall paintings that were found—or to

2. Starr, *Nuzi*, vol. 1, *Text*, 143 and 492. For viewing the borders of the wall paintings see plates 128 and 129 in *Nuzi*, vol. 2.

be more precise, the borders of wall paintings. The borders are extremely important for the claims I am making concerning the location of the events in this story. In these borders, images depict the Egyptian goddess Hathor. She was known at Nuzi. In addition, these Hathor images of the cow with big horns and the lady with the ears of a cow are very much like those in the palace of Amenhotep III in Thebes, and we know that he married two Mitanni princesses. The Egyptians brought Hathor to Nuzi.[3] Whoever came up with our story sent our prince to a place where Hathor was known. The prince's new wife knew all about Hathor and Fates, and so she was able to help the prince with his Fates. Now, this proposed setting for the story is more than a possibility. The story either belongs in Nuzi or some other nearby community.[4]

This story is later than "The Story of the Shipwrecked Sailor" (1800 BCE). It is a story from the New Kingdom.

3. I wonder if the Egyptians brought other gods to this area. It may be helpful to point out that when the prince helps the crocodile overcome the giant, we are reminded of another great battle that took place in the Nile. This was the battle between Horus and Seth. Horus won that battle and was awarded the office of his father, Osirus. In our story the crocodile, or Sobek-Re, is fighting against the giant whose name was probably Teshub, the Hurrian storm god. He is identified with Ba'al in the west, and the Egyptians identified Seth with Ba'al. What this may mean is that Sobek-Re, whose mother, Neith, was always on the side of Horus, wanted the local storm god, Teshub, to know that Horus was in charge here as well as in Egypt.

4. However, I am aware that the Mitanni Kingdom stretched west to the sea, and Hathor was known at Ugarit and Byblos. Steindorff and Seele, *When Egypt Ruled the East*, 50, write: "The tutelary goddess of Byblos was known to the Egyptians and identified with their own Hathor, who in this manner became for the Egyptians the mistress of the Syrian lands." Or we could say the Hurrian lands.

The translation of this story has been more difficult for all translators than the translation of "The Story of the Shipwrecked Sailor," and the end of this story is missing. I have written an ending, which is like the endings in "The Story of the Shipwrecked Sailor" and "The Story of Sinuhe": the hero returns to Egypt for his proper burial. This ending has been placed in brackets. My imagined ending is a happy ending, and therefore I do not call this story "The Story of the Doomed Prince" as others have done in the past. Also I do not use the descriptive title, "The Prince and His Three Fates," which was announced in my first publication of "The Story of the Shipwrecked Sailor." Instead I have followed a great Egyptologist, John A. Wilson, with the title "The Enchanted Prince."

The theme of this story will probably be known to most readers, and certainly to those who have read other tales about contests to see who could win the king's daughter. The tale of Rapunzel has the girl, the tower, the window, and the prince; but other details and the setting are quite different. Alison Lurie writes about the many versions of Rapunzel: "The earliest known appearance of the tale in print occurs in the *Pentamerone* by Giambattista Basile, published in Italy in 1637."[5] Obviously, "The Enchanted Prince" is a witness to this kind of a fairytale at a much earlier time, about three thousand years.

In Egyptian literature from the New Kingdom, when you mention an Egyptian king, queen, any honored person, or sometimes a place, you immediately write, "May

---

5. Lurie, "The Girl in the Tower." This is a delightful and informative article.

he/she *live*, be *prosperous*, and be *healthy.*" In this translation this is abbreviated to "l.p.h."[6]

The text used for this translation can be found in Alan H. Gardiner, *Late-Egyptian Stories.*[7] Gardiner suggestions as to text restorations were usually followed. Damaged sections of the text that have to be restored are put in brackets, but words of clarification are put in parentheses. Parts of the text are underlined, and I have underlined the translation accordingly. Also I have inserted line numbers every five lines. I have been assisted by referring to the translations of Edward F. Wente Jr.[8] and Miriam Lichtheim.[9] In addition, I have received help from many translated examples in Alan Gardiner's *Egyptian Grammar.*[10] This story was told for entertainment; I hope you enjoy it.

The Enchanted Prince

(4,1) <u>Let it be known that there was once</u> a king who did not have a son. [After a while His Majesty, l.p.h., requested] from the local gods a son for himself. They commanded that one should be born for him. During that night he slept with his wife, and yes, [she became] pregnant. After she completed her months for childbearing, a son was

6. The Egyptian scribes just gave the first hieroglyph for the first and third of these three words and the second hieroglyph for the second word. See Figure 1 at the beginning of this chapter.

7. Gardiner, *Late-Egyptian Stories*, 1–9.

8. Wente, "The Tale of the Doomed Prince," 85–91.

9. Lichtheim, "The Doomed Prince," 200–203.

10. Gardiner, *Egyptian Grammar.*

born, and the Hathors[11] came to appoint for him a fate. They said, "He will die by the crocodile, or the serpent, or even the dog."

When the people who were with the child heard this, they repeated it (4,5) to his Majesty, l.p.h. Then his Majesty, l.p.h., became very sad in his heart. So his Majesty, l.p.h., had a [house] of stone [built for his son] out in the desert, and he equipped it with people and with every good thing of the king's palace, l.p.h. The child did not go outside anywhere.

After the child had grown older, he went up to the roof of his castle, and he saw a greyhound; it was following an old man who was walking on the road. He said to his servant, who was beside him, "What is that walking behind the old man who is coming on the road?"

He told him, "That is a greyhound."

The child said to him, "Bring one just like it to me."

Then the servant went to report it (4,10) to his Majesty, l.p.h. His Majesty, l.p.h., said, "Bring for him a frisky puppy, [because of] the grieving of his heart."

So they brought him the greyhound.

Now after [many] days had passed beyond this, the child was fully developed in all his body. He sent to his father saying, "For what purpose am I just sitting here? I am committed to the fate. So let me go. I will do according to my heart, and the God will do what is in his heart."

Then they hitched up a chariot, equipped with (5,1) many weapons. He was given [his servant], and he was ferried across to the eastern land. He was told, "Go wherever your heart desires," and his greyhound was with him. He

11. The Hathor goddesses determined the fates of a newborn.

went north into the desert, following his heart and living on the best of all the desert game.

Finally he reached the Prince of the land of Naharin. Now the Prince of the land of Naharin did not father any one except a daughter, an eligible wife, and he built a house for her; its window was far up, (5,5) seventy cubits from the ground. Then he sent for all the sons of all the princes of the land of Khor, and he told them, "The one who reaches the window of my daughter, she shall be a wife for him."

After many days had passed beyond this and (the princes) were doing their daily practice, the young man passed by them. They took the young man to their house. They bathed him; they gave feed to his team. They did everything for the young man: they anointed him, they bandaged his feet, (5,10) they gave food to his servant, and they talked to him, planning to cause him to speak. "Where do you come from, you good-looking lad?"[12]

He said to them, "I am the son of a chariot officer of the land of Egypt. My mother died, and my father took for himself another wife, a stepmother. She came to hate me, and I ran away, fleeing from her presence."[13] (The princes) embraced him, and they kissed [his whole body].

[After many days had passed beyond this,] he said to (the princes), "What is this that you are doing, [O princes?"

12. This is the question that is asked of the traveler in "Sinuhe" and "The Shipwrecked Sailor."

13. It seems that such questions here and in "Sinuhe" are never answered with the whole truth.

They said to him, "For three months now], we have been here using (6,1) this [time to practice flying. For the one who] reaches [the] window of the daughter of the Prince of the land of Naharin, [he will] give her to him for [a wife.]"

[Then he] said to them, "If I could *enchant my feet*, I would go flying[14] with you."

They went flying according to their daily practice, these princes.

Then [the young man] stood at a distance watching, and also the daughter of the Prince of the land of Naharin [watched] him.

Now after [some time] passed (6,5) beyond this, the young man came to fly with the sons of the princes. He flew and he reached the window of the daughter of the Prince of the land of Naharin. She kissed him; she embraced his whole body.

Then someone went to take the good news to her father, and said to him, "Someone has reached the window of your daughter."

So the Prince asked him saying, "A son of which of the princes?"

And one said to him, "He is a son of a chariot officer. He came fleeing from the land of Egypt [and] from the presence of his stepmother."

14. I think that Wente is correct to translate "enchant." What I do not understand is why no one gives the most basic meaning to the Egyptian *pywt*. It means "to fly." The others could practice flying forever without success. You have to have enchanted feet to fly.

Then (6,10) the Prince of the land of Naharin became exceedingly angry. Then he asked, "Am I to give my daughter to this fugitive from Egypt? Send him back."

Someone came and said [to him], "You must go back to the place from which you came."

But the daughter seized (the young man), and she swore by God saying, "By Pre-Harakhti, if he is taken away from me, I will not eat; I will not drink; I shall die within the hour."

Then the messenger went and reported to her father every [word] that she had said; [her father] sent men to slay him (6,15) right where he was.

The daughter said to [them], "By Pre, if they slay him, at the setting of the sun, I shall be dead. I shall not live an hour more than he."

Then [someone went] to tell her father, and (7,1) [her father had] the [young man, together with his] daughter, [brought before him]. When the [young man came before] him, his value was understood by the Prince. He embraced him, and he kissed his whole body.

He said to him, "Tell me about your story. Note, you have been given to me as a son."

(The young man) said to him, "I am the son of a chariot officer of the land of Egypt. My mother died, and my father took for himself another wife. She came to hate me, and I ran away, fleeing from her presence."

Then (7,5) he gave him his daughter for a wife. He gave him a house with fields as well as cattle and all good things.[15]

---

15. This royal grant reminds us of a similar grant to Sinuhe.

Now after some time had passed beyond this, the young man said to his wife, "I have been given to three fates: the crocodile, the serpent, [or] the dog."

Then she said to him, "So, have the dog that follows after you killed."

He said to her, "[That is] foolishness. I will not have my dog killed, whom I raised from a puppy."

She started to guard her husband with great zeal and did not allow him to go outside walking alone.

Now on the day on which the young man had journeyed from the land of Egypt to wander about, behold the crocodile, (7,10) his fa[te, followed] him [from the land of Egyp]t. The [crocodile] came to live [in the midst] of the lake next to the village where the young man was with [his wife.] Behold, a giant was in [the lake]. The giant would not allow the crocodile to come out for walking, and the crocodile would not allow the giant to come out to walk about. When the sun rose, [they] stood up and fought each other every day for a period of three months.

Now after [many] days had passed beyond this, the young man sat down and made a holiday in his house. After the end (7,15) of the evening breeze, the young man lay down upon his bed, and sleep overcame his body. Then (8,1) his wife filled one [jar with wine; she filled] another jar with beer. Then a [serpent] came forth [from his] hole to bite the young man. But his wife was sitting beside him, and she was not sleeping. So [she put] the [jars] before the serpent, and he drank and became drunk and then lay down belly up. Next [his wife] cut it into pieces with her axe. Then they[16] woke her husband [. . . . . .], (8,5) him,

16. The pronoun "they" is clearly in the text, but with the following break it is difficult.

and she said to him, "Look! *Your God has given one of your fates into your hand. He will protect you [from your fates]."*

[Then he] made an offering to Pre, praising him and extolling his might in the course of every day.

Now after [many days had passed beyond this], the young man went out to walk for pleasure on his place. [His wife] did not [go out with him], but his dog was following him. Then his dog began to speak, [saying, "I am your fate]."

Thereupon, he ran from (the dog). He reached the lake; he went into the [water; he fled from the] dog. (8,10) Then the crocodile [seized] him, and carried him to the place of the giant [. . . . . .]. [The] crocodile [told] the young man, "I am your fate who was made to come after you, but for [three months] now I have been fighting with the giant. Now look, I shall release you. If my [enemy returns] to fight, you [shall] help me kill the giant. For if you see the [giant you will see] the crocodile."

Now after the earth had become bright on the next day, the giant [returned].

End of Text

[The crocodile called to the young man for help. He came running. The crocodile grabbed the giant's feet in his jaws, and the young man with his enchanted feet flew high. He came down hard on the head of the giant and beat him around his eyes. The giant could not see, and the crocodile held his feet and pulled him back. At the same time the young man flew around and hit the giant in the back. The giant fell forward and drowned. The crocodile was tired, and he had been kicked. Then the crocodile said, "Now I will help you with your dog. He is also your fate as he had proclaimed. The crocodile crawled on to the shore, and he caught the dog, and he carried him to the bottom of the lake. The dog was no more, and the crocodile was never seen again.

When the young man reached home, he told his wife what had happened. She said, "I knew that your God would protect you. Now you are free."

"Yes I am free, and perhaps I shall get another puppy."

The young man made offerings to Pre-Harakhti, and he did not forget the crocodile. He made offerings to the crocodile god, Sobek-Re.

Now after many days had passed beyond this,[17] the Prince of the land of Naharin died. The man said to his wife, "We have had a happy life in this land. Now we must take our children, and we will go back to Egypt. There we will live out our last years, and we will be buried in the black earth and journey to the West where there will be good food, good beer, and good music."

This is it, from its beginning to its end, just like most of it was found in a manuscript.] [18]

17. I have underlined this phrase here, since it was underlined elsewhere in the manuscript.

18. This ending is how I think an Egyptian storyteller would have completed it. I am certain that the prince would have to return to Egypt.

3

The Story of the Shipwrecked Sailor

Introduction

It is difficult for any of us to imagine that a story could be 3,800 years old, but "The Story of the Shipwrecked Sailor" qualifies. It was about 3,600 years old when the United States of America was established. Such Egyptian stories predate the great stories of Homer. Cyrus Gordon has said, "Indeed, the whole 'Story of the Shipwrecked Sailor' is to be compared with the episode of the wondrous land of the Phaeacians on which Odysseus was shipwrecked"[1]

This story's serpent or dragon, who could reduce one to a small pile of ashes, has been around in many forms for a long time. Again and again stories of shipwrecks and magnificent islands have thrilled many through the ages, stories like "Sinbad the Sailor" in *A*

1. Gordon, *The Common Background of Greek and Hebrew Civilizations*, 111.

Thousand and One Nights, *Robinson Crusoe*, *The Swiss Family Robinson*, and many more.

During a recent visit to the Museum of Paleontology at the University of Michigan, I met with Professor Philip D. Gingerich, who had recently returned from Egypt. He was able to bring back a specimen of a fifty-million-year-old whale (*Basilosaurus*) that he found on the sands of Egypt west of the Nile in the Faiyum. Professor Gingerich, who found this whale and others, has an ongoing project in the area. This whale has four small limbs and measures sixty feet long.

As soon as I saw this specimen, I realized that ancient Egyptian storytellers, seeing such fossils, probably thought they were serpents. In "The Story of the Shipwrecked Sailor" such a giant "serpent" of thirty cubits in length ruled on a fictional island. In our story, the sailor says, "He placed me in his mouth. He brought me to his lair. He sat me down without hurting me."[2] A skull with jaws of a *Basilosaurus* is also on display in the museum. It is large enough for the ancient storyteller to imagine the "serpent" picking the sailor up in his mouth.

The Egyptians told stories for the purpose of entertainment. "The Story of the Shipwrecked Sailor" is a good example of this. As you enjoy the tale, it makes a point dear to the heart of Egyptian storytellers: It shows *the value of good speech and the persuasiveness of thoughtful words*. This bit of wisdom is the theme of yet an earlier

2. See Wilson, "The Repulsing of the Dragon." Here we encounter another serpent of thirty cubits in length.

story, "The Eloquent Peasant." These works were treasured, and skilled scribes copied them again and again.

The Egyptian language lends itself to colorful expressions; the "sea" is called "the Great Green," and the ship does not "sink," it "dies." Because of such things, I have kept the translation quite literal. Also all additions to the text or restorations are enclosed in brackets.

In "The Story of the Shipwrecked Sailor," a prince has just returned from a mission for the pharaoh. Apparently he did not accomplish this mission with any great success, so the prince is apprehensive about his reception by the pharaoh and the royal court. The chief mate of the ship gives the prince some advice and tries to cheer him up; he even tells him a story from his own experience. The chief mate survived a shipwreck and was able to return to his city where he could live and eventually die in the presence of his family. Unfortunately the prince takes little comfort in the chief mate's story. He does not get the point.

This story goes back to about 1800 BCE. For the hieroglyphic text for this translation, I have used Adriaan de Buck, *Egyptian Reading Book* and Aylward M. Blackman, *Middle-Egyptian Stories.*[3] As usual the translations of Lichtheim and Simpson have been helpful. Lichtheim calls this story a "tale of wonder," and Simpson labels it "a narrative of the unreal."[4] It is a delightful story for all ages. My son, John Fisher, and I have published an illustrated edition of "The Story of the

3. Buck, *Egyptian Reading Book,* 1:100–106; and Blackman, *Middle-Egyptian Stories,* 4–48.

4. Lichtheim, *Ancient Egyptian Literature,* 1:211–15; and Simpson, "The Shipwrecked Sailor."

Shipwrecked Sailor." John's illustrations were a helpful addition to my translation.[5]

Professor Philip D. Gingerich of the University of Michigan found this fifty-million-year-old whale (*Basilosaurus*) in Egypt, west of the Nile in the Fayum, and has an ongoing project in the area. This whale had four small limbs and measures sixty feet long. Ancient Egyptian story-tellers, seeing such fossils, probably thought they were serpents. In *The Story of the Shipwrecked Sailor* (c. 1800 BCE) such a giant "serpent" of thirty cubits in length ruled on a fictional island. This photo was taken at the Museum of Paleontology at the University of Michigan.

5. Fisher and Fisher, *The Story of the Shipwrecked Sailor*.

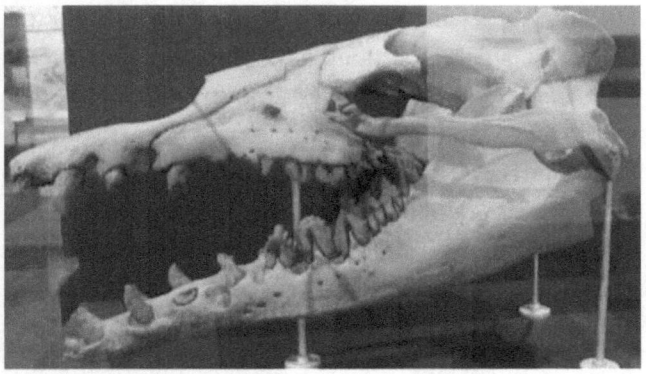

This is a specimen of the skull and jaws of *Basilosaurus*. It is large enough for the ancient storyteller to imagine the "serpent" picking the sailor up in his mouth. In the story, the Sailor says, "He placed me in his mouth. He brought me to his lair. He sat me down without hurting me."

The Story of the Shipwrecked Sailor

(1) <u>The chief mate said</u>,[6] "Take heart, my Prince. Behold, we have reached the palace. The mallet was seized; the mooring-post struck; the prow-rope placed (5) on land. Give praise, and thank God. Each man embraced his fellow; your crew has returned in good condition; there is no loss among our troops. We have left Wawat; we have passed by (10) Senmut.[7] Behold, we have returned in peace, and we have reached our land. Listen to me, O Prince. I make few demands but wash yourself and pour water on your fingers. Then when you are addressed,

6. The Egyptian text has the underline, and I try to do the same in the translation.

7. According to Simpson, "The Shipwrecked Sailor," 51; Wawat is northern Nubia, and Senmet is the island of Biggeh.

(15) you must answer. Speak thoughtfully to the king; you must answer without hesitating. *A man's mouth saves him.*[8] His speech brings forgiveness for him, (20) but do what you want. Speaking to you is wearisome.

"But I shall tell you a similar thing that happened to me. I was going to the mines of the king, and I went (25) down to the Great Green[9] in a ship of a hundred and twenty cubits long and forty cubits wide. One hundred and twenty of Egypt's choice sailors were in it. They watched the sky; they watched the land; (30) their hearts were braver than lions. They could predict a storm before it came and a raging wind before it happened.

"While we were on the great green, a storm came before we reached land. [The storm] brought a wind with it; (35) it repeatedly made a wave, which was eight cubits high. Behold, a [piece] of wood struck me, and then the ship died.[10]

"From those in it, no one remained. I was cast (40) on an island by a wave of the great green. I spent three days alone; my heart was my companion. I lay in the midst of the covering of the trees and kept to (45) the shade.

"Then I stretched forth my two feet in order to find out what I might eat. I found figs and grapes there, many fine leeks, ripe and unripe sycamore figs there, and cul-

8. This is the important theme in Egyptian wisdom.

9. "The Great Green" refers to the sea. It is used of the Mediterranean, but here it is the Red Sea.

10. To say that the ship died is colorful. This expression is also used at Ugarit.

tivated (50) cucumbers. Fish were there and birds; there was nothing that was not in this place.

"I satisfied myself, and I placed [the rest] on the ground, because my arms were so full. I made a fire drill; (55) I started a fire; I gave a burnt offering to the gods.

"Just then I heard a thunderous voice, and I thought, 'It is a wave of the great green.' Trees broke, (60) and the ground trembled. I uncovered my face, and I found it was a serpent; he was coming. He was thirty cubits [long]; his beard was more than two cubits [long]. His body was overlaid (65) with gold, his eyebrows with the best lapis lazuli. He coiled himself forward. Then he opened his mouth to me while I was on my belly before him. He said to me, 'Who brought you? Who brought you, poor fellow, (70) who brought you? If you delay in telling me who brought you to this island, I will introduce you to your [new] self, [since] you will be as ashes, having become as one not seen.'

"You speak to me, [but] I do not understand (75) it. I am before you, [but] I am ignorant."

"So he placed me in his mouth. He brought me to his lair. He sat me down without hurting me. (80) I was whole and nothing was torn from me. Then he opened his mouth to me while I was on my belly before him.

"He asked me, 'Who brought you? Who brought you, poor fellow, who brought you to this island (85) of the great green which is surrounded by water?'

"Finally I answered him; my hands were raised before him. I said to him, 'I went down to (90) the mines as a messenger of the king in a ship of a hundred and twenty cubits long and forty cubits wide. One hundred and twenty of Egypt's choice sailors were in it. (95) They watched the sky; they watched the land; their hearts were braver than lions. They could predict a storm before it came and a raging wind before it happened.

'Each of them, his heart was braver; (100) his arm was stronger than his fellows. There was none who was ignorant. While we were in the great green, a storm came before we reached land. [The storm] brought a wind with it; it repeatedly made a wave, (105) which was eight cubits high. Behold, a [piece] of wood struck me, and the ship died. From those in it, no one remained except me. Behold, I am at your side. I was brought to this island (110) by a wave of the great green.'"

"Then he said to me, 'Do not fear! Do not fear, poor fellow. Do not let your face blanch; you reached me. God has caused you to live; he brought you to this enchanted island.[11] (115) There is nothing that is not in this place; it is full, moreover, of all good things. Behold, you will spend month upon month until you have completed four months in the midst of this island. Then (120) a ship will come from the palace with sailors in it that you know. You shall go with them to the palace; you shall eventually die in your city.

'How joyful is he who tells what he has experienced[12] after the pain has gone away. (125) Let me tell you a similar thing that happened on this island. I was here with my brothers and with children in their midst. All together, [we were] seventy-five serpents, my chil-

11. This is an island of *Ka*, or spirit, and hence enchanted.
12. "What he has experienced" is a translation of "what he has tasted."

dren with my brothers (I will not mention to you a little daughter whom I had obtained by prayer). Then a star (130) fell, and they went up in the flames from it. Now it happened that I was not with them; they were burned. I was not among them. Then I felt dead because of them. I found them, one [pile] of corpses.[13]

'If you are strong and completely subdue your heart, you shall embrace your children; you shall kiss your wife; and you shall see your home. It is more beautiful than anything. (135) You shall reach the palace; you shall be there among your brothers.'"

"Now I was extended out upon my belly; I touched the ground before him. Let me speak to you, 'I shall tell of your nature to the king. I will acquaint him (140) with your greatness. I shall send you two kinds of oil, herbs, incense, and the incense of the temple, which makes content all the gods in it. I shall tell what happened to me from what I have seen of your nature. One will praise god for you in the city before the magistrates of all the land.

'I shall slaughter (145) oxen for you as burnt offerings; I shall sacrifice geese for you. I shall send to you ships laden with all the riches of Egypt as is done for a god who loves people in a far land not known to mankind.'"

"He just laughed at me for what I had said, which seemed foolish in his mind. (150) He said to me, 'You do

---

13. This is an instance of sophisticated narrative, telling a story (the serpent's story) within a story (the chief mate's story) within a story ("The Shipwrecked Sailor"). Compare this technique in the Arabic *A Thousand Nights and a Night*.

not have much myrrh or all kinds of incense; I am the ruler of Punt, and myrrh belongs to me. That oil which you spoke of bringing, it is the main thing of this island. It will happen that when you have left this place, you will never see this island again; it will have become water.'"

"Later that ship (155) came as he had foretold beforehand. I went and placed myself up in a tall tree; I recognized those that were in it. When I went to report it, I found him, and he knew it. He said to me, 'In health, in health, poor fellow, to your home and you will see your children. Cause my name to be fair in your city. Behold, that is my due (160) from you.'

"Then I put myself on my belly; my hands were raised before him, and he gave me a load of myrrh, oil, herbs, incense, spice, perfume, eye paint, giraffe tails, wood, incense, (165) tusks of ivory, greyhounds, monkeys, baboons, and all kinds of riches. I loaded them on the ship, and I placed myself on my belly to thank him. Then he said to me, 'Behold, you will reach the palace in two months. Behold, you will embrace your children. You will be young and vigorous at the palace, and you will be buried.'[14]

"I went down to the shore (170) in the vicinity of this ship. After calling to the crew, which was on the ship, I gave praise on the shore to the lord of this island. Those in the [ship] did the same. We sailed north to the palace of the king.

---

14. All Egyptians wanted to be buried in their homeland. Jacob desired his body to be returned to Canaan for burial with his kin (Genesis 49:29–32).

"We reached the palace in two months, just like all he had said. So I went in before the king. (175) I presented the gifts I brought from the island. He praised god for me before the magistrates of all the land, and I was made a chief mate and endowed with two hundred persons. 'Look at me! After (180) I was endowed with land [and] after I considered what I had experienced, you should listen to my mouth. Behold, it is good for people to listen.'"

Thus the Prince said to me, "Don't use such skill, my friend. Who would give water (185) to a goose at dawn that will be slaughtered that morning?"

This is it, from its beginning to its end, just like it was found in a manuscript of a scribe with skilled fingers, Imeny son of Imena'a—Life! Prosperity! Health!

4

The Journey of Wen-Amon

Introduction

"The Journey of Wen-Amon" was produced about one thousand years after Egypt gave us "The Story of Sinuhe." During the last part of the reign of Ramses XI (about 1090 to 1080 BCE), the rule of Egypt was divided between Heri-Hor of Thebes, in the south, and Ne-su-Ba-neb-Ded (Smendes) of Tanis, in the north. Wen-Amon was from Thebes, and he was sent to Byblos in Phoenicia to buy cedar for the divine barque of Amon-Re.[1] I take the position along with many others that this story or report concerns a real journey. In any case it gives us interesting and important information about Egypt and Phoenicia at this time. There is one section of the story, which is badly damaged, and in addition, we do not have the ending. But

1. This information is available in many places, e.g., Wilson, *The Culture of Ancient Egypt*, 289–92; Lichtheim, *Ancient Egyptian Literature*, 2:224; and Wente, "The Report of Wenamon," 142. Wilson's comments on Wen-Amon's travels contain great insight.

the fact that the report exists is usually taken as proof that Wen-Amon did return to Egypt and wrote this account of his travels.

It is difficult to find anyone who seems interested in the meaning of the name Wen-Amon. Perhaps this is because the meaning is obvious to most translators. But what is interesting to anyone who also works with Hebrew, Phoenician, Ugaritic, and Babylonian (or Akkadian) is that the pattern is typical. The first element (*Wen* in this case) means "there is/are" or "to exist," and the second element is of course a divine name. So we have the meaning "Amon exists/lives," and this is helpful when dealing with the Northwest Semitic examples, which follow this pattern:

- Phoenician, *'ithba'al*
- Hebrew, *'eshba'al*
- Ugaritic, *'ishba'al* (related to the phrase *'ith ba'al*: "Ba'al lives")
- Babylonian, *'i-shi-ba'al.*

The first element in all of these means "to exist." Many scholars have made the mistake of seeing this first element as meaning, "man."[2] This mistake is probably caused by the false analogy with *'ishbosheth*, "Man of shame."[3]

In the following translation, the text I use is from Alan H. Gardiner's *Late-Egyptian Stories* (62–76). I will

2. Astour, *Hellenosemitica*, 91–92 n. 4, has seen the same pattern among Cretan names in an Egyptian text. One of them he wrongly translates as "Man of Horus." I would translate it as "Horus lives."

3. Cyrus Gordon (*UT*, 111, 367, 368) and Albright (*Archaeology and the Religion of Israel*, 113) do not make this mistake.

give the line numbers for every five lines (1, 5, 10, etc.), and I will include my notes. Also I will underline the places in the translation where the original text is underlined, and my additions will be in parentheses and the restorations in brackets.

Needless to say I have been helped many times by the translations of John Wilson, Edward F. Wente Jr., and Miriam Lichtheim. I have learned from them, and I depart from their work only when the evidence forces my hand. They have made some mistakes, and I am certain that I have made my share. But our work is a real adventure, and it is a lot of fun to be able to get close to the author of this report. We cannot get inside his head, but we can get close to him.

The Journey of Wen-Amon

(1,1) <u>Year 5, the 4th month of the summer, day 16:</u>[4] the day on which Wen-Amon, the Elder of the Portal of the Temple of Amon, [Lord of the Thrones] of the Two Lands, departed in order to obtain timber for the great and noble barque of Amon-Re, King of the Gods, which is upon the [river, whose name] is User-het-Amon.

On the day when I reached Tanis at the place [where Ne-su-Ba-neb]-Ded[5] and Tanet-Amon were, I gave them the letters of Amon-Re, King of the Gods, and they (1,5) had them read in their presence. Then they said, "Will do!

---

4. This date cannot be reconciled with the date given in 1,6. Something is wrong.

5. This is "Smendes," followed by his wife's name.

Yes! Will do according to the word of Amon-Re, King of the Gods, our [Lord]."

I remained until the beginning of the 4th month of summer, day 1[6] in Tanis. Na-su-Ba-neb-Ded and Tanet-Amon sent me along with the ship's captain, Mengebet. I went down to the great sea of Syria[7] in the first month of summer, day 1. I arrived at Dor, a town of the Tjeker,[8] and Beder, its prince,[9] had fifty loaves of bread, one jug of wine, (1,10) and a hindquarter of a steer brought to me. Then a man from my ship fled (after) he stole one [vessel] of gold [worth] five *deben*,[10] four vessels of silver worth twenty *deben*, and a sack of eleven *deben* of silver. [A total of what] he [stole]: gold, five *deben*, (and) silver, thirty one *deben*.

I got up the (next) morning, and I went to where the prince was. I said to him, "I have been robbed in your harbor. You are the prince of this land; you are its judge, who should find my valuables.[11] Indeed, the valuables

6. Again this date does not work with the date in 1,1 unless it is a year later like *rnpt* (year) 6.

7. The Egyptian *ḫ3rw* (Khor) is usually translated "Syria," but it is related to the Hurrians. On this point see Wilson, *ANET*, 258 n. 4; and Wilson, *The Burden of Egypt*, 257.

8. The Tjeker were one of the Sea Peoples.

9. The Egyptian word for "prince" is *sr*. This is of course related to Hebrew *śar*, Ugaritic *shar* and Akkadian *sharru*. The Egyptian *shrr/shari* or "small/child" is also related to this group in that it can be used in a phrase meaning, "the son of a king," see Erman and Grapow, *Wörterbuch der Aegyptischen Sprache*, 4:526. For this word we also have Ugaritic *ṯrr* and Akkadian *sherru*.

10. This is a measure of weight: approximately 91 grams during the New Kingdom.

11. The Egyptian word means, "silver," but it stands for all of

belong to Amon-Re, (1,15) King of the Gods, Lord of the Two Lands; they belong to Ne-su-Ba-neb-Ded; they belong to Heri-Hor, my lord and the other great ones of Egypt. They belong to you; they belong to Weret; they belong to Mekmer; they belong to Zakar-Ba'al, the prince of Byblos."

He said to me, "Whether you are important or are excellent,[12] (no matter); look, I am not able to understand how to answer what you have said to me. If this thief belonged to my land, who went down to your ship to steal your valuables, I would replace them until they have[13] (1,20) found your thief, whatever his name may be. But the thief who robbed you, he belongs to you. He belongs to your ship. Spend a few days here with me. I will search for him."

I spent nine days, and I was moored in his harbor. Then I went to him, and I said to him, "Look, you have not found my valuables. [Please send] me with the ships' captains, with those who go to sea."

He said to me, "Be silent!"

> *The next five lines are broken (1,24–28a), and they are difficult to restore. Beder, the prince of Dor, apparently tells Wen-Amon that he should stay in the harbor at Dor until his stolen goods are found, but he is impatient and leaves for Tyre. There are still broken places in 1,29–36. This translation begins again at 1,28b.[14]*

---

the valuable things. Wente and Lichtheim translate "money" which seems a bit anachronistic.

12. This indicates that he is an elite.

13. Here I follow Gardner's note.

14. Wente attempts a translation of all of this. For 1,24–28a, I

I left Tyre at dawn . . . Zakar-Ba'al, the prince of Byblos . . . (1,30) ship. I found thirty *deben* of silver in it. I seized it . . . your silver until they have found [my valuables or the thief,][15] who stole *them*. You have not stolen, but I will take it. But as for you[16] . . .

Then they[17] departed, and I celebrated [in] a tent on the shore of the sea (by) the harbor of Byblos. [I hid (?)] Amon-of-the-Road, and I put his possessions within him.[18]

Then the [prince] of Byblos sent to me saying,[19] "[Depart from] (1,35) [my] harbor."

Then I sent to him saying, "Where [should I go?] . . . If [you can find (?)] some transportation by ship, I could be taken back to Egypt."

I stayed twenty-nine days in his [harbor]. He spent time daily sending to me saying, "Depart from my harbor."

Now while he made an offering to his gods, the god took one of his high-ranking boys from the elite group of boys, and he made him ecstatic. He (i.e., the boy) said to him, "Bring up [the] God. Bring the messenger who

can only give you the following words: . . . find . . . hear [my words] . . . until they have gone to search for their thief . . . the harbor . . . [Ty]re.

15. As restored by Gardiner.

16. Again restored by Gardiner. Apparently he took this silver from the Tjeker, which causes him a lot of trouble later on.

17. I suppose that "they" refers to the Tjeker.

18. "Amon-of-the-Road" was a portable image of Amon that would help him on his mission.

19. Egyptian *rdd*, "saying" is parallel to Hebrew *le'mor*, "saying" (the same preposition plus infinitive "to say"). This is used again and again in subsequent lines (e.g., 1,43).

carries him. (1,40) Amon sent him; it is he who made him come."

While the entranced one was mad that night,[20] I found a ship; it was headed for Egypt. I loaded everything of mine into it. While watching for the darkness (I was) saying, "(When) it descends I will load the god, so that another eye will not see him."

Then the harbormaster came to me saying, "Wait until morning, so says he, namely,[21] the prince."

I said to him, "Was it not you who spent time coming to me daily saying, 'Depart from my harbor'? Are you not saying wait tonight (1,45) in order to allow the ship that I found to depart, and then you will come to say, 'Go! Get out!'?"

He went and told it to the prince, and the prince sent (a message) to the captain of the ship saying, "Stay until morning, so says he, namely, the prince."

When morning came, he sent and brought me up, and the God remained in the tent where he was on the shore of the sea. I found him (in) his upper room, leaning his back against a window, and the waves of the great sea of Syria were breaking (1,50) behind his head.[22] I said to him, "Praised be Amon."

And he said to me, " How many are the days[23] since you came from where Amon is?"

20. Note the parallel of the Hebrew Bible referring to prophets as "mad" (e.g., 1 Samuel 10:9; 2 Kings 9:11; Jeremiah 29:26; and Hosea 9:7).

21. Here I follow Gardiner's note on 65a.

22. This is a remarkable description. It is a beautiful portrait, and as such it is rarely seen in these ancient stories.

23. Again I follow Gardiner's note, 66a.

And I said to him, "Five months of days till now."

And he said to me, "Well, you are truthful. So where are the documents of Amon, which were in your hand? Where are the letters from the High Priest of Amon, which were in your hand?"

And I said to him, "I gave them to Ne-su-Ba-neb-Ded and Tanet-Amon." He was exceedingly angry.

And he said to me, "Now see here, seeing that documents (and) letters are not in your hand, where is the cedar ship that Ne-su-Ba-neb-Ded gave to you? Where is (1,55) its Syrian crew? Did he not give you to the captain of a foreign ship in order to kill you and throw you to the sea?[24] With whom would they seek the God? Not with me. And you, with whom would they seek you? Not with me."[25] Thus he said to me.

So I said to him, "Wasn't it a ship of Egypt? Now it is Egyptian crews, which sail under Ne-su-Ba-neb-Ded. He does not have Syrian crews."

And he said to me, "Aren't there as many as twenty ships here in my harbor? They have shipping protection granted by Ne-su-Ba-neb-Ded. As this (place) called Si-don (2,1), the other (place) that you passed, aren't there another fifty ships there? These ships are protected by Werket-El, and they ship to his house."[26]

24. This is so much like the book of Jonah that I wanted to translate, "throw you to *hayam*" (Hebrew, "the sea"; see Jonah 1:15). In Egyptian the same word is used for "sea."

25. The other translations do not include "Not with me" after these questions. It is difficult. I base my translation on the information from Erman and Grapow, *Wörterbuch der Aegyptischen Sprache*, 5:595 and 596.

26. On Werket-El I follow Wilson's translation in *ANET*, 27.

So, I was silenced at this crucial time.

Then he answered (and) said to me,[27] "What are you doing? Traveling on account of what mission?"

And I said to him, "I am making (this) trip to bring back the timber for the great and noble barque of Amon-Re, King of the Gods. What your father did, what (2,5) your grandfather did, you will do it as it was done." I said to him.

And he said to me, "In truth, they did it! If you pay me for doing it, I will do it. Truly, when they carried out this mission, they were paid. Pharaoh, l. p. h., sent six ships loaded with Egyptian goods, and they were unloaded into their storehouses. But, what is it that you have brought to me, yes, to me?"

Then he ordered his ancestors' *Scrolls of the Days*,[28] and he had them read in my presence. They found (entered) one thousand *deben* of silver (and) all sorts of thing in his scrolls. (2,10) So he said, to me, "If the ruler of Egypt were my Lord, I would be his servant. He would not have

---

Also see Wente, "The Report of Wenamon," 147, note 13, for other options, e.g., Warkatara. This merchant was probably an Asiatic and living in Egypt.

27. Both verbs together ("answered and said") occur in many places in the Hebrew Bible. For example, we have this in Genesis 18:27; 40:18; and in the introductions to each speech in the great debate in Job 3–26.

28. This is like the Hebrew title for chronicles of kings: *sefer divrey hayyamim*, "the scroll of the words/acts of the days." See 1 Kings 14:29. Aage Bentzen says, "The kings of pre-Israelite Canaan had their *books* in which the *acts of their ancestors* were written. This is a very important fact to be taken into account in the present discussion of the significance of oral tradition." He goes on to refer to this passage in Wen-Amon. See Bentzen, *Introduction to the Old Testament*, 1:245. He also refers to Wen-Amon in four other places.

to send silver (and) gold saying, 'Do the commission of Amon.' A royal gift[29] would not be brought as they did for my father. As for me, yes, me, I am not one of your servants, and I am not a servant of the one who sent you. If I call, crying out to the Lebanon,[30] the sky opens, and the timber is put here on the shore of the sea. Give[31] (2,15) me the sails that you brought to steal away your ships, which will transport your timber to [Egypt]. Give me ropes that you brought [to bind the cedar timber] that I am to cut down in order to make for you [. . .] I will make for you sails (for) your ships, because the heavy load must be protected or you will die in the middle of the sea.[32] Look, Amon made thunder in the sky, when in his time, he put Seth beside him.[33] Indeed, Amon (2,20) has established

29. This word in Egyptian is *mrk* and is the Semitic *mlk*.

30. The Egyptian for Lebanon is *rbrn*. This is interesting. The first *r* of course is written for the "L." However the second *r* stands for "n." This is strange, but this is also the case in the stela of Seti I where the Egyptian scribe writes the final *n* in Beth-Shan with an *r* (see line 16). For this, see my comments in Fisher, *The Minority Report*, 150. The text of Seti I is in Rowe, *The Topography and History of Beth-Shan*, 27.

31. See Gardiner's *Grammar*, §336 for this spelling of the imperative.

32. Wilson is probably on the right track. He says in *ANET*, 27 n. 22, "Zakar-Baal's argument is not clear here." But, if he takes the sails and ropes, Wen-Amon will not be able to slip away without the proper financial arrangements. Also it seems that the sails will be made in a manner that would be helpful during a storm. This seems to protect the interests of Zakar-Baʿal and at the same time issue a warning to Wen-Amon.

33. Seth was identified with Baal. They were both storm gods. Who knows? Baal just might see to it that Wen-Amon would be punished.

all the lands.[34] When he established them, he established first the Land of Egypt from which you have come. Thus craftsmanship came from it to reach the place where I am, and learning[35] came from it to reach the place where I am. What are these silly trips, which they made you take?"

And I said to him, "It is not true. These are not silly trips that I am on. There is no ship on the River that does not belong to Amon. The sea is his, and the Lebanon is his of which you say, 'It is mine.' He made (2,25) the growing plot for User-het-Amon, the Lord of every ship. Truly, it was Amon-Re, King of the Gods, who said to Heri-Hor, my Lord, 'Send him.'[36] So he had me come, carrying this great God. But look, you have made this great God spend these twenty-nine days moored in your harbor. Did you not know? Isn't he here? Isn't he the one who has always been?[37] You are stationed (here) to facilitate the commerce

34. This reminds one of Deuteronomy 32:8–9. Note Smith's translation based not on the Masoretic text but on a Dead Sea Scroll fragment and the Septuagint:

> When the Most High (Elyon) allotted peoples for inheritance,
> When he divided up humanity,
> He fixed the boundaries for peoples,
> According to the number of the divine sons:
> For Yahweh's portion is his people,
> Jacob his own inheritance.

This can be found in Smith, *The Origins of Biblical Monotheism*, 48.

35. Or wisdom. It is interesting that the Egyptian root *sbi* has to do with teaching, learning, and wisdom; but with a different determinative it can mean a "rebel." This entire statement of Zakar-Baʿal is an amazing admission of the importance of Egypt.

36. Wente correctly translates "him" even though the text has "me."

37. He should have listened to the prophetic voice of the boy (see above: 1,39–40).

of the Lebanon with Amon, its Lord. As for your constant saying that the former kings sent silver and gold, so be it, but if they had possessed life (and) health, they would not have sent these things. (2,30) But they sent these things instead of life (and) health to your fathers. Now as to Amon-Re, King of the Gods, he is the Lord of this life (and) health, and he was the Lord of your fathers. They spent their lifetimes making offerings to Amon. And you, so it is, you are the servant of Amon. If you say, 'Will do, will do[38] for Amon,' and you carry out his commission, you will live, you will prosper, you will be healthy, and you will be good for your entire land and your people. Do not covet for yourself anything belonging to Amon-Re, (King) of the Gods. 'Truly, a lion king loves his possessions!' Now have your scribe brought to me. (2,35) I will send him to Ne-su-Ba-neb-Ded (and) Tanet-Amon, the officers whom Amon put in the north of his land, and they will have everything sent. I shall send him to them saying, 'Have it brought until I have come (again) to the south, and I shall have all, yes all,[39] of the debt that has not been paid brought to you.'"[40] Thus I spoke to him.

He put my letter in the hand of his messenger. Then he loaded the keel beam, the bow post, and the sternpost along with another four hewn timbers: a total of seven. He had them sent to Egypt.

38. Wente uses this sign for a repeat in his translation. It was also used in 1,5.

39. Just as in 1,5 there is the repeat sign in the text; see 2,37.

40. The speeches are getting longer. I am reminded of the speeches in the Joseph story.

His messenger, who had gone to Egypt, returned to me in Syria in the first month of winter. Ne-su-Ba-neb-Ded (and) Tanet-Amon sent (2,40) four jars (and) one *kakmen* vessel of gold, five jars of silver, ten garments of royal linen, ten *ḥrd* garments of fine linen, five hundred rolls of smooth papyrus, five hundred ox-hides, five hundred ropes, twenty sacks of lentils, and thirty baskets of fish. She[41] sent to me: five garments of fine linen, five *ḥrd* garments of fine linen, one sack of lentils, and five baskets of fish.

The prince rejoiced, and he assigned three hundred men and three hundred oxen, and he put supervisors over them, to have them cut down the trees. So, they cut them, and they were left there during the winter. In the third month of summer, they dragged them (to) the shore of the sea, and the prince came, and he stood upon them. He sent to me (2,45) saying, "Come." Now, when I presented myself near him, the shadow of his lotus-fan fell on me. Pen-Amon,[42] a butler, who belonged to him, pushed me saying, "The shadow of the pharaoh, i.e., your Lord, has fallen on you."[43]

41. This is Tanet-Amon.

42. This is an Egyptian name. It means "He of Amon."

43. As Wilson suggests, the meaning of what the butler says is lost on us. I can only make attempt to understand the word "shadow," but this does not really explain what the butler was really saying. The "shadow" has to do with "protection" or "influence." If this is related to a great god, all is well, but if to a divine enemy, it is not good. Here I am thinking of the "shadow of Mot" (the West Semitic god of Death). Note Job 10:20–22:

> Are not my days few? Desist!
> Stand away from me, and let me smile a little
> Before I go (and I will never return)

(The prince) was angry with him, saying, "Leave him."

As I came (again) beside him, he answered (and) said[44] to me, "Look, the commission, which my fathers first carried out, also I have done it, but you have not done for me what your fathers did for mine, (nothing) from you. See, the last of your timber, and it has been stacked. Do as my heart (wishes). Come and load it. Will they not give it to you? (2,50) Do not come (just) to consider the terror of the sea. If you look at the terror of the sea, you will see my own (as well). Indeed, I have not done to you what was done to the messengers of Kha'em-Waset. After they spent seventeen years in this land, they died where they were."

And he said to his butler, "Take him there. Show him their tomb[45] in which they are lying; they are there."

And I said to him, "Don't show it to me. As for Kha'em-Waset, he sent to you men as messengers. He was a man himself.[46] You do not have before you one of

---

To [the] netherworld of darkness, to the shadow of Mot,
A netherworld of darkness like gloom,
The shadow of Mot and chaos;
[The netherworld] was as bright as gloom.

But this does not explain why he said that the shadow of Pharaoh fell on him.

44. See n. 27 above for this use of "answered and said."

45. The word for "tomb" does not have the correct determinative. The one it has would suggest that the meaning should be "lifetime." See Erman and Grapow, *Wörterbuch der Aegyptischen Sprache*, 1:222; on 221 they have "gravestone" with the correct determinative, but in 2:49 and in Gardiner's note more options are presented and give us good reason to read "tomb."

46. He was not a pharaoh, only a man.

his messengers. Yet you say, 'Go and see your companions.' Isn't it true that you should rejoice? (2,55) Then you should have a stela made for you, and you should say on it: 'Amon-Re, King of the Gods has sent to me Amon-of-the-Road, his messenger, l.p.h., along with Wen-Amon, his human messenger, after timber for the great and noble barque of Amon-Re, King of the Gods. I cut it down. I loaded it. I readied it (for) my ships (and) my crews. I caused them to reach Egypt in order for me to request fifty years of life from Amon over and above my fate.' And it will happen that after some time, a messenger will come from the land of Egypt, and he will know writing. He will read your name on the stela. You will receive water (in) the West like all the Gods who are (2,60) there."[47]

And he said to me, "A great testimony of words is this you have said to me."[48]

And I said to him, "As for the many things, which you have said to me, if I reach the sanctuary[49] where the High Priest of Amon is, and he sees your commissions as your (completed) commissions, they will bring a profit for you of something."

And I went (to) the shore of the sea, to the place where the timber was stacked, and I saw eleven ships that

47. The Egyptian word for "there" really means "here," but we translate "there." The West is the place where the dead go, and this mentions the offering of water for the dead, and the speaker somehow speaks from that place.

48. I think Wente's translation brings out the irony of this statement: "That is quite a wordy bit of testimony you have said to me." Action may be better than words, but we need to remember the Egyptian's love of great speech.

49. I have translated "place" as "sanctuary." I know that with other languages in this area the word place refers to a sanctuary.

had come in from the sea. They belonged to the Tjeker (who) said, "Arrest him! Do not allow a ship to take him to the land of Egypt."

Then I had to sit down to weep. The scribe of the prince came out to me, (2,65) and he said to me, "What's with you?"

And I said to him, "Haven't you seen the migrating birds go down[50] to Egypt two times? Look at them. They are traveling from[51] the cool water. Until what transpires will I be left here? Have you not seen those who have come again to arrest me?"

And he went, and he told it to the prince. And the prince started to weep because of the words that were spoken to him, for they were miserable. He ordered his scribe to come out to me, and he brought me two jugs of wine and one ram.[52] Then he sent to me Ta-net-Ne, an Egyptian singer, who was with him, saying (to her), "Sing to him! Don't allow fear for his mind's plans." And he came to me, (2,70) saying, "Eat! Drink! Don't allow fear for your mind's plans. You shall hear everything that I have to say tomorrow."

When morning came, he summoned his assembly.[53] He stood in their midst, and he said to the Tjeker, "Why have you come?"

50. Here I am tempted to translate "go south." In any case Wen-Amon is complaining that he has been gone for more than a year.

51. The preposition *r* is usually translated "to," but it can be "from" as well. Obviously the birds are moving away from the cold. Either way this is an interesting and realistic observation.

52. See Erman and Grapow, *Wörterbuch der Aegyptischen Sprache* 1:38 for *iyr* from Hebrew *ʾyl* or "ram."

53. "Assembly" is from Egyptian *mwʾdw*, and this is parallel to the Hebrew *moʿed*.

They said to him, "We have come after the double-damned ships that you are sending to Egypt along with our enemy."

He said to them, "I cannot arrest the messenger of Amon in the midst of my land. I will send him forth, and you can go after him in order to arrest him."

So, he loaded me and sent me away from there, from the harbor of the sea, and the wind drove me to the land of (2,75) Alashiya.[54]

Then the citizens of the town came out against me to kill me, but I forced my way and escaped to the place where Hatiba, the princess of the town was. I found her as she was coming out of one of her houses, and she was entering another. So I greeted her, and I said to the people, who were standing near her, "Isn't there one of you who understands Egyptian?"

And one of them said, "I understand."

And I said to him, "Tell my lady that I have heard, as far away as Thebes, the place where Amon is, a saying that 'lies are created in every town, but truth is made known in the land of Alashiya.' But are lies told here every day?"[55]

And she said, "O, what is it (2,80) you have said?"

And I said to her, "If the many waters are angry, and the wind casts me on the land where you are, you should not allow them to take me in order to kill me. I am a messenger of Amon. Look, as for me, they will search for me every day. As for the crew of the prince of Byblos, whom they are seeking to kill, won't their lord find ten crews belonging to you and kill them as well?"

54. This is Cyprus.

55. Note the later adage: "Cretans are always liars" (Titus 1:12).

So she had the people summoned, and they stood there. Then she said to me, "Spend the night."

(We do not have the rest of the story, but he probably made it back to Egypt and wrote this account. But then after a night with Hatiba, he could have delayed his plans for some time.)

5

A Dialogue between a Man and His *Ba*[1]

Introduction

This fascinating story is extremely difficult to translate because the beginning of the prologue is missing. This creates problems in translating what follows. Because of the variety of interpretations and the resultant controversy, it is important for the reader to look at several translations. Miriam Lichtheim refrains from a detailed discussion of this work because it would require too many pages.[2] My translation is not meant to replace the work of others, but it was essential for me to translate this work in order to enter the discussion and to understand the problems.

---

1. Egyptian *Ba* is usually translated "soul."
2. Lichtheim, *Ancient Egyptian Literature*, 1:163.

I have been assisted by the translations of John A. Wilson,[3] R. O. Faulkner,[4] and Miriam Lichtheim,[5] and I have used the text provided by R. O. Faulkner in *The Journal of Egyptian Archaeology*.

Our text appears to be from the Twelfth Dynasty (1990–1785 BCE), but John Wilson would say that the story is older. It may be from the transition to the Middle Kingdom (about 2000 BCE), when there was a great deal of chaos.[6]

This story is important for me, because I have recently translated the Book of Job.[7] There are many similarities between these two works. There are similar ways of expressing the sufferings and the delights of humans, and the basic structure of prose plus poetry plus prose cannot be overlooked. In both books there is a longing for death by a man, who is struggling to pull himself out of an unjust quagmire.

A Dialogue between a Man and His *Ba*

We do not know how much of the Prologue is missing, and the first extant lines of this text only give us a few words and disconnected phrases. This translation begins with the last part of line 3.[8]

3. Wilson, "A Dispute over Suicide."

4. Faulkner, "The Man Who Was Tired of Life," in *The Literature of Ancient Egypt*, 201–9.

5. Lichtheim, *Ancient Egyptian Literature*, 1:163–69.

6. Wilson, "A Dispute over Suicide," 405.

7. Fisher. *The Many Voices of Job*.

8. The words: "You to say . . . not partial . . . payment. Their tongues are not partial."

Prologue

Then I opened my mouth to my [*Ba*] that I might answer what he[9] had said:

(5) This is too great for me today; my *Ba* will not speak with me. Moreover it is too great to be [exaggerated]. It is as if I am alone.[10] My *Ba* should [not] go away; he should attend me on this. [. . .] he should not take away [. . .] in my body with a network of rope. It will not (10) be that he is able to depart on the painful day. Look, my *Ba* wrongs me. I do not listen[11] to him. I will drag myself toward death—not having come to it—and will throw myself on the fire to burn. [. . .] (15) May he approach [me] (on) the painful day; may he stand on the other side, as does the one who prays.[12] This is the one who goes forth; he does bring himself. My *Ba* is too foolish to lower the pain in life, but holds me back from death[13] before I come to it. Sweeten the West[14] (20) for me. Is that too painful? This is a journey, that is, this life, and (note) the trees: they fall. You, tread on evil; put down my misery.

9. "He" refers to the *Ba* or soul. Most translations use "it," which works in English but objectifies the soul. In Hebrew, *nephesh* ("soul/being") is feminine.

10. Literally, "I am idle."

11. "Listen" in most languages implies "to obey."

12. "The one who prays" is a suggestion. Most leave this word as "unknown."

13. "Holds me back" Others translate *ihm*, "leads me toward."

14. "The West" is the heavenly abode of the immortal. Why did they call this the West? Because the burial grounds along the Nile were literally west of the Nile on higher ground.

Judge me, O Thoth,[15] who gives rest to the gods.

Defend me, O Khons,[16] (25) who is a true scribe.

Hear my words, O Re,[17] who calms the sacred sun-barque.

Defend me, O Isdes,[18] in the holy chamber.[19]

For my suffering is too heavy of a burden; it is stronger than I am. It is pleasant that the (30) gods defend the secrets of my body.

What my *Ba* said to me:

Are you not a man? You are alive. What do you gain from your complaining about life like a lord of wealth?

I said:

I have not gone, that is, to the earth. Surely if you depart, (35) care will not be given to you. Every criminal says, "I will seize you." You are dead though your name lives. Yonder is a place of rest, the way of the heart. A home: this is the West. A rowing[20] [. . .]. If my *Ba* [listens]

15. He is the god of wisdom and writing.

16. A moon god.

17. The sun god.

18. A god tied closely to Thoth.

19. He seeks judgment from the divine court. This poem points to the Day of Judgment. See Montet, *Everyday Life in Egypt*, 302–8. The judgment included the weighing the deceased's heart on one side of a balanced scale with a statue of Truth (the feather of truth) on the other side. If this test is passed, the person is declared by Thoth to be "just of voice," which means that the person is qualified for immortality. This was done in the "Hall of the Two Truths." This reminds one of Job's seeking legal judgment. Perhaps, *Job I* (in Job 31:35–37), and *Job II* (in Job 9, 13, and 23).

20. The break here is unfortunate, but in the burial ritual there is one stage where the body is put in a boat and the boat is rowed across the Nile to the West.

to me, an innocent (40) [m]an,[21] his heart is in accord
with me, he will be fortunate. I will make him reach the
West like one who is in his pyramid at whose burial one
stood upon his ground.[22]

> I shall make a shelter over your corpse;
> You will scorn another *Ba* (45) in weariness.
> I shall make a shelter—now it will not be cold;
> You will scorn another *Ba* who is hot.
> I shall drink water at a flowing stream where I made
> shade.
> You will scorn another *Ba* who is hungry.

If you hold (50) me back from death in this way, you
will not find where you can rest in the West. Be patient, my
Ba (and) my brother, until my heir has appeared, who will
make offerings, who will stand on the grave on the day of
burial,[23] who will prepare a bed (55) for the necropolis.

**My *Ba* opened his mouth to me that he might an-
swer what I had said:**

If you are thinking of burial, it is heartbreaking.
This is bringing tears by making a man miserable; this is
taking a man from his house and throwing (him) on the
hill.[24] Never again will you go up to see (60) the sun.[25]

21. The phrase "an innocent man" is literally "not a man of
crime."

22. The text has "my ground," which seems to be a mistake. This
phrase has a parallel in Job 19:25: "But as for me, I know that my
avenger lives, and a guarantor by [my] grave will stand" (or: "on the
dirt will stand").

23. Again we have the heir standing on the grave as we noted in
Job 19:25.

24. The hill is the necropolis west of the Nile.

25. When you are dead, you will not be coming back to see the
sun.

The builders constructed with red granite the chambers within good pyramids with fine construction, but when the builders became gods,[26] their offering stones were destroyed like the weary ones who died on the riverbank for lack of (anyone) above ground,[27] (65) (and with these) the floods realized its goal and the sunshine as well. The fish at the bank of the water talk to them. Listen to me! Behold, it is good for people to listen. Pursue the good days and forget worries.[28]

A poor man plowed his plot.[29] He loaded his harvest (70) in the ship's hold and traveled (along the lake) by his towing. His feast days approached, and he saw the coming of darkness and a north wind. He was watchful in the boat. As the sun set, (he) came out with his wife (and) his children but was defeated upon the lake encircled in (75) the night with crocodiles. Finally, he sits down sharing his voice saying, "I am not weeping for that mother, who will not come again from the West for another time upon earth. I grieve on account of her children, broken in the egg, who have stared at the face of the crocodile-god (80) (and) they have not lived."

A poor man asked for an early meal. His wife said to him, "It is for supper." He went outside to [. . .] for a while; he returned to his house, and he was like another man.

26. They became gods after their death.

27. They did not have any living relative to observe the proper rituals.

28. This sounds like the Harper's Song from the tomb of King Intef, "Make Holiday." See Lichtheim, *Ancient Egyptian Literature*, 1:197.

29. Here the *Ba* begins the first of two stories that he tells to illustrate the points that he has just made. Life is not easy.

His wife was skilled in dealing with him, but he did not listen to her. He [. . .]³⁰ (85) deeply felt by the servants.

Then I opened my mouth to my *Ba* that I might answer what he had said:³¹

[Part1]

> Look, my name stinks!³²
> Look, more than the stench of bird shit
> On summer days when the sky is burning.
>
> Look, my name stinks!
> Look, <more than the stench> of a catch of fish
> On a fishing day when the sky is burning.
>
> Look, my name stinks!
> Look, more than the stench of bird shit,
> More than a mound of reeds with waterfowl.
>
> Look, my name stinks!
> Look, more than the stench of catching fish,
> More than the marsh-pools (95) where they fished.

---

30. He probably killed her or beat her.

31. This is a long response containing four poems. The structure of prose plus poetry plus prose now becomes obvious (as in Job).

32. His name is all that he has. See Montet, *Everyday Life in Egypt*, 305, for a discussion of chapter 30 in the *Book of the Dead*. In this chapter there is a prayer to ensure that the heart will be true on the Day of Judgment, and a request: "Let my name not stink, speak no falsehood against me in the presence of the god!" This man is worried about the Day of Judgment.

Look, my name stinks!
Look, more than the stench of crocodiles,
More than where the crocodiles rest on the shores.

Look, my name stinks!
Look, more than a wife,
Who tells lies to them (about) a man.[33]

Look, (100) my name stinks!
Look, more than a perfect child,
Of whom it is said, "He is the flesh of his (father's) rival."

Look, my name stinks!
Look, <more than> the town of a king,
Which is rebellious, seeing his back (is turned).

[Part 2]

To whom can I speak today?
Brothers are evil;
The friends of today do not love.

To whom (105) can I speak today?
Hearts are rapacious;
Everyone robs his brother's goods.

33. She is like the wife in the Egyptian work "The Story of the Two Brothers" and the story of Joseph and Potiphar's wife (Genesis 39:1–18).

<To whom can I speak today?>
Mildness has perished;
Strength attacks everyone.

To whom can I speak (110) today?
The calm face is evil;
Goodness is thrown to the ground everywhere.

To whom can I speak today?
One should enrage another by his doing evil;
He makes everyone laugh (at) his crime.

To whom can I speak today?
Men plunder;
Every one robs his brothers.

To whom can I speak today?
The criminal is an intimate;[34]
A brother with whom one worked has become (115)
    an enemy.

To whom can I speak today?
Yesterday is not remembered;
Now nothing is done for him who used to help.

To whom can I speak today?
Brothers are evil;
One goes to foreigners for loyalty of the heart.

---

34. "Intimate" is literally "one who enters the heart."

To whom can I speak today?
Faces perish;
Everyone has a downcast face toward (120) his
    brothers.

To whom can I speak today?
Hearts are rapacious;
There is no heart of man on which one can rely.

To whom can I speak today?
There are no truthful people;
The land is left to the doers of evil.

To whom can I speak today?
The intimate is gone;
One comes to an unknown (125) to complain to him.

To whom can I speak today?
There are no contented people;
That one with whom he used to go does not exist.

To whom can I speak today?
I am burdened, even I, with wretchedness
From the absence of an intimate.[35]

To whom can I speak today!
Wrong roams the earth; (130)
An end to it does not exist.

35. Here is a lonely man.

[Part 3]

Death is in my face today
<Like> the recovery of a sick man,
Like going outside again after being confined.

Death is in my face today
Like the fragrance of myrrh,
Like sitting under sail on a windy day.[36]

Death is in my face today (135)
Like the fragrance of lotus,
Like sitting on the shore of the Land of
    Drunkenness.[37]

Death is in my face today
Like a trodden water path,
Like the return of men to their homes from warfare.

Death is in my face today
Like a clearing of the sky,
Like a man who is trapping (140) for what is not
    known to him.

Death is in my face today
Like men wanting to see their homes
(After) spending many years in captivity.

---

36. Here the determinative is not correct for "sail" but rather it implies "shade"; but "sail" seems to make better sense.

37. Like getting to go out on a picnic.

[*Part 4*]

> Finally, in truth, he who is yonder will be a living
>> god,[38]
>
> Punishing the crime of the one who did it.
>
> Truly, he who is yonder will stand in the sacred sun-
>> barque;
>
> He will give the choicest gifts (145) therein to the
>> temples.
>
> Truly, he who is yonder will be a sage,
>
> Who will not be prevented from petitioning Re when
>> he speaks.

Epilogue

What the *Ba* said to me:

Put your complaining aside, my comrade, my brother.
Make offerings on the brazier; (150) and cling to life like
<I> have told you. Love me here.[39] Reject the West, and
desire that you may reach the West when your body joins
the earth.[40] I will alight after you are weary. Then we shall
make an abode together.

Colophon

It is finished (155) from beginning to end as it was found
in writing.

---

38. It is after death that one becomes immortal and divine. This
is also the case at Ugarit. See Lewis, *The Cults of the Dead in Ancient
Israel and Ugarit*.

39. This could be "Love me now!" This is a great command.

40. That is, in a natural death.

Conclusion

Alfred North Whitehead's comment on the task of modern scholars has long intrigued me. While discussing the growth of civilization and the slow "shift in human mentality," he says, "The record has been written up by editors with the mentality of later times. Thus the task of modern scholars is analogous to an endeavor to recover the histories of Denmark and Scotland from a study of *Hamlet* and *Macbeth*."[1] But the task is greater than Whitehead suggests, because it is not just the histories of the past that we must recover, but also the portraits of later times that are supplied by those editors with the mentality of later times. Gary Rendsburg has developed a similar idea in his essay on "The Genesis of the Bible."[2] Rendsburg compares the creation of English literature with that of Hebrew literature. In both cases playwrights or editors use real places and real people, which the audience or reader knows. For example, in the book of Genesis the stories of the patriarchs are narrated, but the "shadow of David and Solomon is evident throughout."[3] Rendsburg says that this is the

1. Whitehead, *Adventures of Ideas*, 52–53.

2. Rendsburg, "The Genesis of the Bible," 11–30.

3. Fisher, "The Patriarchal Cycles," 65. Here I explain my view of "observable facts" and "actual facts" as this pertains to the patriar-

same technique that Arthur Miller uses in *The Crucible*, in which a known past is narrated, but the point of the story was to speak to the present—to speak to McCarthyism. His next example is taken from the movie *M*A*S*H*. The story takes place during the Korean War, but it was really an antiwar movie about Vietnam.

In *Genesis, A Royal Epic*,[4] I have shown that the stories of the Patriarchs that were rehearsed at the tomb dealt with people, names, and events that were known to the audience. But bringing these stories together in a Royal Epic was for the purpose of uniting Judah and Israel in the time of David. It was also one way of creating the line of David and reinforcing the point that David was the legitimate king. Again Whitehead's definition of our task is important. We need to be able to understand the situation and the intent of later editors.

To appreciate Egyptian stories fully, we need to understand the story and at the same time understand the intent of the storyteller. In Egypt, "The Story of Sinuhe" was a great adventure story. Though it is a novel, it gives us real information about Egypt's foreign relations, about the people in the far north, and about Sinuhe. Ancient Egyptians told this story to entertain, but they continued to tell it again and again to make the point that a person,

---

chal cycles. The stories as preserved by the minstrels may only give us a few "observable facts," but when these stories were put together in a Royal Epic, the "actual facts" or actual occasions of experience on the part of editors and the people of the new and united Israel were abundant. Also see note 5 below and the reference to the work of John B. Cobb Jr. on this topic.

4. Fisher, *Genesis, A Royal Epic*, 206–10. This example has to do with Genesis 38.

who may have been a great success in a foreign land, always wanted to return to Egypt for proper burial.

"The Enchanted Prince" is another type of adventure story. Also this story is the first in a long series in the history of literature of similar fairy tales. But the Egyptians inserted in this story a didactic element. Fate for the Egyptians was not something that was set in concrete. Though the protagonist had to speak of his Fates, there were always ways of escape. This was the hearer's delight.

"The Shipwrecked Sailor" does not give us much historical information about the distant past, but we learn that "A man's mouth saves him." The power of persuasive speech was important to the Egyptians, as we have noted in "The Eloquent Peasant." The didactic element could always be used to deal with a later problem. The story within the story makes it clear how stories were used.

"The Journey of Wen-Amon" is not a novel, but it was used to inform the people of Egypt that even when Egypt was weak its past remained important in the eyes of many such as the prince of Byblos. As a report or memoir it may contain fictional elements, but even so, it is important for the historians search for observable facts and actual facts.[5] In most of these stories, we find that the actual facts or actual occasions of experience belong to those who edited and those who heard these stories. Their experience was enjoyable, and they learned something as well.

---

5. Cobb, "Ontology, History, and Christian Faith," 270–87. An "observable fact" is what a neutral observer would have seen if he had been there. Hence at first Cobb called such facts "hypothetical." An "actual fact" has to do with an actual occasion of experience in any individual subject.

"A Dialogue between a Man and His *Ba*" may not give us many observable facts; we do not know much about the man, but it does reveal to us, and especially in the poetry, this man's unbearable condition. I imagine that many of those who heard this story listened with understanding. They had been there. This literature reveals a great deal concerning the soul of these people.

Flashes of Freedom

Whitehead is the one who influenced me concerning the importance of what I have called minority opinions, and which he calls great ideas, insights, or "flashes of freedom."[6] Such ideas are necessary for civilization to evolve. Both Greek and Hebrew voices have been instrumental in providing "flashes of freedom" for "*A Program for Discontent*"[7] or perhaps for our day *An Inconvenient Truth*. I think we must live in the world of our research at least part time, and with bold imagination based upon that research, we can advance what Whitehead started. It is important to see how "flashes of freedom" work in the general evolution of civilization. Whitehead's *Adventures of Ideas* is one of my favorite books. He deals with "The History of the Human Race" but is quick to say, "the Human Race must experience its own history. It cannot be written in its total variety."[8] This is true, and we could add that the task is not only impossible but even a partial history is too difficult for any one historian. In my opinion

6. Whitehead, *Adventures of Ideas*, 22, 49, and 171.
7. Ibid.,12.
8. Ibid., 3.

Whitehead gives too much credit to the Greeks and the Hebrew prophets for flashes of freedom and not enough credit to the east Mediterranean world.[9]

In the introduction to chapter 2 and "The Enchanted Prince," I suggested a probable setting for this story was at Nuzi, and because of the wall paintings in the palace at Nuzi, it was clear that Egypt played an important role in the lives of these Hurrian citizens. Based on the Nuzi texts, what can we say about life in that city? Edward Chiera, Cyrus H. Gordon, and Martha A. Morrison[10] all agree that from the Nuzi tablets we know that the women in Nuzi had the same rights as the men. Women and men were equals in the social and the economic life of the community. Why did the Hurrians see men and women as equals? This was not the usual view in their part of the world, but it seems to be the case that they influenced the Egyptians. According to Wilson,[11] the importance of women was stressed during the Amarna Age in Egypt. He even calls this a "strong feminism." I think the Mitanni women in the harem of Egypt probably spoke out on the question of equality. One princess from Mitanni is reported to have brought with her an entourage of three hundred seventeen women.[12] According to John A. Wilson,[13] Thut-mose

9. Ibid., 8. Here he says, "the Near East is only important for this discussion in its function of the origin and the background of modern Europe."

10. Chiera made a great contribution to the study of the Nuzi Texts; see his *They Wrote on Clay*; Gordon, *Adventures in the Nearest East*, 105–20; Morrison, "A Continuing Adventure," 31–35.

11. Wilson, *Culture of Ancient Egypt*, 203 and 214.

12. This is a bit more than Gideon's three hundred men in Judges 7:8 but falls one short of Abram's 318 in Genesis 14:14.

13. Wilson, *The Culture of Ancient Egypt*.

III (1490–1436 BCE) had troubles with the Mitanni Kingdom (or Naharin), but Thut-mose IV (1406–1398 BCE) married a Mitanni princess. Amen-hotep III (1398–1361 BCE) married two princesses from Mitanni, but perhaps Tadu-Kepa, daughter of Tushratta, came into the harem of Akh-en-Aton (1369–1353 BCE). The Egyptians were in contact with Naharin. Why relate all of this? It is because Whitehead seems to overlook the contribution of the Egyptians in the Amarna Age and particularly that of Akh-en-Aton (Whitehead's Akhnaton).[14] However, it appears to be the case that Wilson's "strong feminism" was a flash of freedom during Akh-en-Aton's reign, and it was ignited by the Hurrians.

I would like to close with a poem, which I present in the style of John Dryden, who was a great translator.

Flashes of Freedom

Not much has changed in five millenniums.
Technology has, a bit with humans.
Once we came ashore and to the heights climbed,
Our ascent became a saw-tooth flat line.

There were hints of social justice around;
They were not widespread, and faint was the sound.
Ubiquitous injustice was alive,
And noise of practitioners was rife.

14. Whitehead, *Adventure of Ideas*, 49.

If we can cross the language barrier,
And if we can hurdle the many years,
To bridge rivers of misunderstanding,
There is an adventure for the taking.

A great idea spells flashes of freedom.
All must line up: body, soul, and persuasion.
There has to be discontent and true critique.
It takes hope and time, no place for the meek.

Did social justice help the pharaoh's plan?
A loyal follower was his demand.
The New Empire's love was for expansion,
And human rights were not in its mission.

Later, there was a creative advance.
In the Amarna Age, Egypt came through.
Or Akh-en-Aton, the rebel, came through.
There were flashes of freedom for a few.

Women were a part of the public life.
Pharaoh's love was shown for daughters and wife.
How did this change for women come about?
The harem wives from Mitanni spoke out.

The Mitanni Kingdom was far away.
There, men and women had equality.
These Hurrians are best known from Nuzi.
Modern Kirkuk is near ancient Nuzi.

Nuzi texts are windows without curtains.
We see Kizaya, who won in the court
Her right to wed her lover, Arteya.
She was freed from the match with Mannuya.

The adventurous gave us these insights.
They looked beyond safe limits and their plight.
Their learning was essential for nurture,
But imagination brought adventure.

It restores vigor to know these people,
People, who with programs of discontent
Retained a vibrant hope for the future.
Our civilization needs such people.

Their flashes of freedom are to be treasured.
Lightning is fertile, not to be measured.
Ours to remember: "In any Kingdom,
Altar, Greed, and Empire kill flashes of freedom.

Bibliography

Albright, W. F. *Archaeology and the Religion of Israel.* 3rd ed. Baltimore: Johns Hopkins University Press, 1953.

Astour, Michael C. *Hellenosemitica: An Ethnic and Cultural Study in West Semitic Impact on Mycenaean Greece.* Leiden: Brill, 1967.

Bentzen, Aage. *Introduction to the Old Testament.* 2 vols. in 1. Copenhagen: Gad, 1957.

Blackman, A. M. *Middle-Egyptian Stories.* Bibliotheca Aegyptiaca II. Brusselles: Édition de la Fondation Égyptologique Reine Élisabeth, 1972.

Buck, Adriaan de. *Egyptian Reading Book.* Vol. I. Leyden: Nederlandsch Archaeologisch Instituut Voor Het Nabije Oosten, 1948.

Burkert, Walter. *Lore and Science in Ancient Pythagoreanism.* Translated by Edwin L. Minar Jr. Cambridge: Harvard University Press, 1972.

Chiera, Edward. *They Wrote on Clay: The Babylonian Tablets Speak Today.* Edited by George G. Cameron. Phoenix Books. 15th Phoenix edition. Chicago: University of Chicago Press, 1966.

Cobb, John B., Jr. "Ontology, History, and Christian Faith." *Religion in Life* (1965) 270–87.

Drioton, Étienne, and Jacques Vandier. *L'Égypte.* "CLIO," Les Peuples de L'Orient Méditerranéen II. Paris: Presses Universitaires de France, 1952.

Edgecomb, Diane. *A Fire in My Heart: Kurdish Tales.* World Folklore Series. Westport, CT: Libraries Unlimited, 2007.

Erman, Adolf, and Hermann Grapow, editors. *Wörterbuch der Aegyptischen Sprache.* 7 vols. Berlin: Akademie, 1926–1963.

Faulkner, R. O. "The Man Who Was Tired of Life." In *The Literature of Ancient Egypt,* edited by William Kelly Simpson, 201–9. New edition. New Haven: Yale University Press, 1973.

Bibliography

———. "The Man Who Was Tired of Life." *Journal of Egyptian Archaeology* 42 (1956) 21–40.

Fisher, Loren R. "An International Judgment." In *The Claremont Ras Shamra Tablets*, edited by Loren R. Fisher, 11–22. AnOr 48. Rome: Pontificium Institutum Biblicum, 1971.

———. *Genesis, A Royal Epic*. Willits, CA: Fisher Publications, 2000

———. *The Many Voices of Job*. Eugene, OR: Cascade Books, 2009.

———. *The Minority Report*. Willits, CA: Fisher Publications, 2004.

———. "The Patriarchal Cycles." In *Orient and Occident: Essays Presented to Cyrus H. Gordon on the Occasion of His Sixty-fifth Birthday*, edited by Harry A. Hoffner Jr., 59–65. Alter Orient und Altes Testament 22. Neukirchen-Vluyn: Neukirchener, 1973.

Fisher, Loren, and John Fisher. *The Story of the Shipwrecked Sailor*. Willits, CA: Fisher Publications, 2004.

Gardiner, Alan H. *Egyptian Grammar*. 2nd ed. London: Oxford University Press, 1950.

———. *Egypt of the Pharaohs: An Introduction*. Oxford: Clarendon, 1961.

———. *Late-Egyptian Stories*. Bibliotheca Aegyptiaca I. Brussells: Édition de la Fondation Égyptologique Reine Élisabeth, 1932.

Gopnik, Adam. "Prisoner of Narnia." *The New Yorker*, November 21, 2005, 88–93.

Gordon, Cyrus H. *Adventures in the Nearest East*. London: Phoenix House, 1957.

———. *Before the Bible*. New York: Harper & Row, 1962.

———. *The Common Background of Greek and Hebrew Civilizations*. Norton Library. New York: Norton, 1965.

———. "Homer and the Bible." *HUCA* 26 (1955) 43–108.

———. *Ugaritic Literature: A Comprehensive Translation of the Poetic and Prose Texts*. Scripta Pontificii Instituti Biblici 98. Rome: Pontificium Institutum Biblicum, 1949.

———. *Ugaritic Textbook*. AnOr 38. Rome: Pontificium Institutum Biblicum, 1965.

Gordon, Cyrus H., and Gary A. Rendsburg. *The Bible and the Ancient Near East*. 4th ed. New York: Norton, 1997.

Hartshorne, Charles. *Omnipotence and Other Theological Mistakes*. Albany: State University of New York Press, 1984.

Hertzberg, Hans Wilhelm. *I & II Samuel*. Translated by J. S. Bowden. Old Testament Library. Philadelphia: Westminster, 1964.

Hoffner, Harry A. Jr. "A Hittite Analogue to the David and Goliath Contest of Champions." *Catholic Biblical Quarterly* 30 (1968) 220–25.

Homan, Michael M. "Beer and Its Drinkers: An Ancient Near Eastern Love Story." *Near Eastern Archaeology* 67 (2004) 84–95.

Lewis, C. S. *The Allegory of Love: A Study in Medieval Tradition*. 1936. Reprint, Oxford: University Press, 1959.

Lichtheim, Miriam. *Ancient Egyptian Literature*. Vol. 1. Berkeley: University of California Press, 1975.

———. *Ancient Egyptian Literature*. Vol. 2. Berkeley: University of California Press, 1976.

———. "The Dispute between a Man and His *Ba*." In *Ancient Egyptian Literature* 1:163–69. Berkeley: University of California Press, 1975.

———. "The Doomed Prince." In *Ancient Egyptian Literature* 2:200–203. Berkeley: University of California Press, 1976.

Lurie, Alison. "The Girl in the Tower." *The New York Review of Books*, May 1, 2008, 40–43.

Montet Pierre. *Everyday Life in Egypt*. Translated by A. R. Maxwell-Hyslop and Margaret S. Drower. London: Arnold, 1958.

Moran, William L. *The Amarna Letters*. Baltimore: Johns Hopkins University Press, 1992.

Morrison, Martha A. "A Continuing Adventure: Cyrus Gordon and Mesopotamia." *Biblical Archaeologist* 59 (1996) 31–35.

Pope, Marvin H. *Job*. 3rd ed. Anchor Bible 15. Garden City, NY: Doubleday, 1973.

Pritchard, James B. *Ancient Near Eastern Texts*. 3rd ed. Princeton: Princeton University Press, 1969.

Rainey, A. F. "The World of Sinuhe." *Israel Oriental Studies* 2 (1972) 369–408.

Rendsburg, Gary A. "The Genesis of the Bible." Inaugural lecture delivered at Rutgers University, New Brunswick, NJ, October 28, 2004. New Brunswick, NJ: Allen and Joan Bildner Center for the Study of Jewish Life, Rutgers University, 2005.

Rowe, Alan. *The Topography and History of Beth-Shan* Philadelphia: The University Press for the University of Pennsylvania Museum, 1930.

Simpson, William Kelly. "The Shipwrecked Sailor." In *The Literature of Ancient Egypt: An Anthology of Stories, Instructions, and Poetry*, edited by William Kelly Simpson, 50–56. New ed. New Haven: Yale University Press, 1973.

———. "The Story of Sinuhe." In *The Literature of Ancient Egypt: An Anthology of Stories, Instructions, and Poetry* edited by William Kelly Simpson, 57–74. New ed. New Haven: Yale University Press, 1973.

Smith, Mark S. *The Origins of Biblical Monotheism: Israel's Polytheistic Background and the Ugaritic Texts.* Oxford: Oxford University Press, 2001.

Starr, Richard F. S. *Nuzi.* 2 vols. Harvard-Radcliffe Fine Art Series. Cambridge: Harvard University Press, 1939 and 1937.

Steindorff, George, and Keith C. Seele. *When Egypt Ruled the East.* 2nd ed. Chicago: University of Chicago Press, 1957.

Taylor, Henry Osborn. *The Mediaeval Mind.* 2 vols. 4th ed. Cambridge: Harvard University Press, 1949.

Vaux, Roland de. *Ancient Israel.* Translated by John McHugh. New York: Scribners, 1961.

Wente, Edward F., Jr. "The Report of Wenamon." In *The Literature of Ancient Egypt: An Anthology of Stories, Instructions, and Poetry*, edited by William Kelly Simpson, 142–55. New ed. New Haven: Yale University Press, 1973.

———. "The Tale of the Doomed Prince." In *The Literature of Ancient Egypt: An Anthology of Stories, Instructions, and Poetry*, edited by William Kelly Simpson, 65–91. New ed. New Haven: Yale University Press, 1973.

Whitehead, Alfred North. *Adventures of Ideas.* New York: Free Press, 1967.

Wilson, John A. *The Burden of Egypt: An Interpretation of Ancient Egyptian Culture.* Oriental Institute Essay. Chicago: University of Chicago Press, 1951.

———. *The Culture of Ancient Egypt.* Phoenix Books. Chicago: University of Chicago Press, 1956.

———. "A Dispute over Suicide." In *ANET*, 405–7.

———. "The Journey of Wen-Amon to Phoenicia." In *ANET*, 25–29.

———. "The Repulsing of the Dragon." In *ANET*, 11–12.

———. "The Story of Sinuhe." In *ANET*, 18–22.

Index of Authors and Scholars

Albright, W. F., 55, 93

Astour, Michael C., 55, 93

Bentzen, Aage, 62, 93

Blackman, Aylward M., 7, 45, 93

Buck, Adriaan de, 45, 93

Burkert, Walter, xi, 93

Chiera, Edward, 31, 89, 93

Cobb, John B., Jr., 86–87, 93

Drioton, Étienne, 93

Edgecomb, Diane, 31, 93

Erman, Adolf, 4, 57, 61, 67, 69, 93

Faulkner, R. O., 74, 93

Fisher, John, ii, xiii, 45–46

Fisher, Loren R., ix, xiv, 1–2, 6–7, 21, 46, 63, 74, 85–86, 94

Gardiner, Alan H., 4, 11, 20, 23, 35, 55, 59–60, 63, 67, 94

Gingerich, Philip D., 44, 46

Gopnik, Adam, x–xi, 94

Gordon, Cyrus H., xiii, xiv, 17–18, 43, 55, 89, 94

Grapow, Hermann, 4, 57, 61, 67, 69, 93

Hartshorne, Charles, 1, 94

Hertzberg, Hans Wilhelm, 16, 94

Hoffner, Harry A., Jr., 16, 94, 95

Homan, Michael M., 25, 95

Lewis, C. S., x–xi, 84, 95

Lichtheim, Miriam, 1, 5–6, 11, 24, 35, 45, 54, 56, 58, 73–74, 78, 95

Lurie, Alison, 34, 95

Montet Pierre, 19, 76, 79, 95

Moran, William L., 95

Morrison, Martha A., 89, 95

Pope, Marvin H., 95

Pritchard, James B., 95

Rainey, Anson F., 6, 10, 95

Rendsburg, Gary A., 1, 85, 94

Rowe, Alan, 63, 76, 95

Rummel, Stan, xiii, xiv

Seele, Keith C., 33, 96

Simpson, William Kelly, 6, 11, 15, 17, 19, 36, 45, 47, 93, 95, 96

Smith, Mark S., 64, 96

Starr, Richard F. S., 32, 96

Steindorff, George, 33, 96

Taylor, Henry Osborn, xi, 96

Vandier, Jacques, 93

Vaux, Roland de, 16, 96

Ward, William A., ix, xiii

Wente, Edward F., Jr., 35, 38, 54, 56, 58, 62, 64–65, 68, 96

Index of Authors and Scholars

Whitehead, Alfred North,
     85–86, 88–90, 96
Wilson, John A., 2, 6, 8, 26, 34,
          44, 54, 56–57, 61, 63,
          66, 74, 89–90, 96

Index of Ancient Documents

EGYPTIAN

The Autobiography of Harkuf, 5
The Autobiography of Weni, 5
The Book of the Dead, 79
*A Dialogue Between a Man
    and His Ba*, 3, **73–84**
The Eloquent Peasant, 2, 45, 87
The Enchanted Prince, 2,
    30–42, 87, 89
The Journey of Wen-Amon, vi,
    3, **54–71**, 87
The Story of Sinuhe, 1–3, **5–29**,
    32, 34, 37, 39, 54, 86
*The Story of the Shipwrecked
    Sailor*, xi, 3, 10, 23, 26,
    33–34, 37, **43–53**, 87
The Story of the Two Brothers,
    80
Tel el-Amarna Tablet #286, 17

UGARITIC

RS 1957.1   7

HEBREW BIBLE

Genesis
14:14   89
18:27   62
29:1   9
29:26   14
35:19–20   21
38   86
38:1–9   23
39:1–18   80
40:18   62
41:14   28
41:42   28
45:5   11
49:29–32   19, 52
50:20   11

Deuteronomy
32:8–9   64

Judges
7:8   89

Index of Ancient Documents

1 Samuel

10:9	60
17	17
27:5–6	14

2 Samuel

9:1–13	14
14:30–31	14
18:18	21

1 Kings

11:18	14
11:19	7
14:29	62
15:12	7

2 Kings

9:11	60
10:13	7

Job

	3–4, 74, 79
1:3	10
3–26	62
9	76
10:1	4
10:20–22	6
13	76
19:25	77
23	76
31:35–37	76

Psalms

89:7	12

Proverbs

30:22a	16

Jeremiah

29:26	60

Hosea

9:7	60

Jonah

1:15	61

∽

NEW TESTAMENT

Titus

1:12	70

GREEK

Iliad

3	17
7	17